DATE DUE

APR 3 0 2007	APR 1 1 2009
AUG 0 7 2007	APR 2 5 2009
OCT 1 7 2007	DEC 0 1 2009
OCT 3 1 2007	AUG 0 1 2011
OCT 3 1 2007	SEP 1 5 2011
NOV 1 5 2007	OCT 2 2 2011
MAY 0 8 2008	NOV 0 1 2011
	NOV 2 9 2012
OCT 2 9 2008	Jul 7, 2013
NOV 2 4 2008	NOV 1 8 2013
FEB 2 0 2009	
MAR 0 9 2009	DEC 1 7 2016
MAR 2 8 2009	MAR 0 8 2018
	AUG 0 2 2018

Writing the Critical Essay

THE DEATH PENALTY

An OPPOSING VIEWPOINTS® Guide

William Dudley, *Book Editor*

Bruce Glassman, *Vice President*
Bonnie Szumski, *Publisher, Series Editor*
Helen Cothran, *Managing Editor*

OPPOSING
VIEWPOINTS®
SERIES

GREENHAVEN PRESS
An imprint of Thomson Gale, a part of The Thomson Corporation

THOMSON

GALE

Detroit • New York • San Francisco • San Diego • New Haven, Conn. • Waterville, Maine • London • Munich

For more information, contact
Greenhaven Press
27500 Drake Rd.
Farmington Hills, MI 48331-3535
Or you can visit our Internet site at http://www.gale.com

LIBRARY OF CONGRESS CATALOGING-IN-PUBLICATION DATA

The death penalty / William Dudley, book editor.
  p. cm. — (Writing the Critical Essay: An Opposing Viewpoints Guide)
   Includes bibliographical references and index.
  ISBN 0-7377-3208-3 (lib. : alk. paper)
   1. Capital punishment—United States. 2. Essay—Authorship—Problems, exercises, etc.
I. Dudley, William, 1964– . II. Series.
  HV8699.U6D43 2006
  179.7—dc22

2005045993

Printed in the United States of America

CONTENTS

Section Two: Model Essays and Writing Exercises

Section Three: Supporting Research Material

Examining the state of writing and how it is taught in the United States was the official purpose of the National Commission on Writing in America's Schools and Colleges. The commission, made up of teachers, school administrators, business leaders, and college and university presidents, released its first report in 2003. "Despite the best efforts of many educators," commissioners argued, "writing has not received the full attention it deserves." Among the findings of the commission was that most fourth-grade students spent less than three hours a week writing, that three-quarters of high school seniors never receive a writing assignment in their history or social studies classes, and that more than 50 percent of first-year students in college have problems writing error-free papers. The commission called for a "cultural sea change" that would increase the emphasis on writing for both elementary and secondary schools. These conclusions have made some educators realize that writing must be emphasized in the curriculum. As colleges are demanding an ever-higher level of writing proficiency from incoming students, schools must respond by making students more competent writers. In response to these concerns, the SAT, an influential standardized test used for college admissions, required an essay for the first time in 2005.

Books in the Writing the Critical Essay: An Opposing Viewpoints Guide series use the patented Opposing Viewpoints format to help students learn to organize ideas and arguments and to write essays using common critical writing techniques. Each book in the series focuses on a particular type of essay writing—including expository, persuasive, descriptive, and narrative—that students learn while being taught both the five-paragraph essay as well as longer pieces of writing that have an opinionated focus. These guides include everything necessary to help students research, outline, draft, edit, and ultimately write successful essays across the curriculum, including essays for the SAT.

Using Opposing Viewpoints

This series is inspired by and builds upon Greenhaven Press's acclaimed Opposing Viewpoints series. As in the parent series, each book in the Writing the Critical Essay series focuses on a timely and controversial social issue that provides lots of opportunities for creating thought-provoking essays. The first section of each volume begins with a brief introductory essay that provides context for the opposing viewpoints that follow. These articles are chosen for their accessibility and clearly stated views. The thesis of each article is made explicit in the article's title and is accentuated by its pairing with an opposing or alternative view. These essays are both models of persuasive writing techniques and valuable research material that students can mine to write their own informed essays. Guided reading and discussion questions help lead students to key ideas and writing techniques presented in the selections.

The second section of each book begins with a preface discussing the format of the essays and examining characteristics of the featured essay type. Model five-paragraph and longer essays then demonstrate that essay type. The essays are annotated so that key writing elements and techniques are pointed out to the student. Sequential, step-by-step exercises help students construct and refine thesis statements; organize material into outlines; analyze and try out writing techniques; write transitions, introductions, and conclusions; and incorporate quotations and other researched material. Ultimately, students construct their own compositions using the designated essay type.

The third section of each volume provides additional research material and writing prompts to help the student. Additional facts about the topic of the book serve as a convenient source of supporting material for essays. Other features help students go beyond the book for their research. Like other Greenhaven Press books, each book in the Writing the Critical Essay series includes bibliographic listings of relevant periodical articles, books, Web sites, and organizations to contact.

Writing the Critical Essay: An Opposing Viewpoints Guide will help students master essay techniques that can be used in any discipline.

Background to Controversy: The Death Penalty Debate in America

Capital punishment has been part of American history dating back to the first English colonies in the 1600s. The colonies adopted English law traditions that included a long list of crimes punishable by death: murder, treason, theft, robbery, rape, and arson, among others.

By the time of the American Revolution of 1776, some people were questioning the death penalty. One of the earliest death penalty opponents was Benjamin Rush, a physician and signer of the Declaration of Independence. Rush argued that the death penalty was an unfortunate legacy from England and its monarch, and that the new republic of America should not condone premeditated killing by the government. He wrote a number of books and pamphlets calling for its abolition. "The punishment of murder by death is contrary to reason, and to the order and happiness of society," Rush wrote.

Rush and other death penalty abolitionists had mixed success in their campaign to end or limit the death penalty in America. The state of Pennsylvania in 1794 developed the concept of "degrees" of murder, restricting capital punishment to deliberate and premeditated murder in the "first degree." Other states soon followed Pennsylvania's lead by reducing the number of capital crimes or, in some cases, abolishing capital punishment altogether. Michigan became the first U.S. state to outlaw the death penalty in 1846, followed by Rhode Island and Wisconsin. But many states, especially in the South, retained the death penalty for a wide variety of crimes (including slave insurrection). Other state legislatures went back and forth, abolishing the death penalty only to reinstate it due to public fears about crime.

U.S. Executions Stop and Resume

In the twentieth century death penalty opponents challenged capital punishment in federal court as a violation of the "cruel and unusual punishment" ban of the Eighth Amendment to the Constitution. Their efforts almost led the United States to abolish the death penalty. In 1967 the Supreme Court suspended all scheduled executions while they debated the issue. The justices ruled in 1972 in the case of *Furman v. Georgia* that the death penalty was unconstitutional because it was applied inconsistently and randomly. The ruling nullified existing death sentences and voided state and federal death penalty statutes. America's movement away from the death penalty mirrored a global trend. In 1997 South Africa became the forty-second nation since World War II to abolish capital punishment.

Accused witch Stephen Burroughs awaits execution by hanging in Salem, Massachusetts, in 1692. Capital punishment has been a part of American history since colonial times.

Executions in the United States Since 1976, by Region

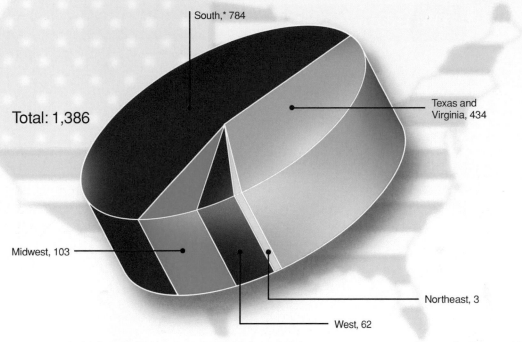

South,* 784

Texas and Virginia, 434

Total: 1,386

Midwest, 103

Northeast, 3

West, 62

Source: Death Penalty Information Center, www.deathpenaltyinfo.org.

*Except for Texas and Virginia

Most Western industrialized nations had by then legally or effectively abandoned the death penalty.

In the United States, however, a different path was ultimately taken. Many states acted within a few years of the *Furman* decision to revise their death penalty laws to address the Supreme Court's concerns. Four years after *Furman*, the Supreme Court ruled in *Gregg v. Georgia* to let most of the new laws stand. A main reform was that death sentences could not be automatically given following the conviction of a crime, but instead required an additional jury's decision in which aggravating and mitigating circumstances of the crime were weighed. Thirty-eight states have enacted death penalty statutes following *Furman*. Public opinion polls have consistently shown that the American people support the death penalty, sometimes by a 2-1 margin. But the renewed and seemingly secure status of the death penalty in America has not prevented ongoing disagreement about its ethics and efficacy.

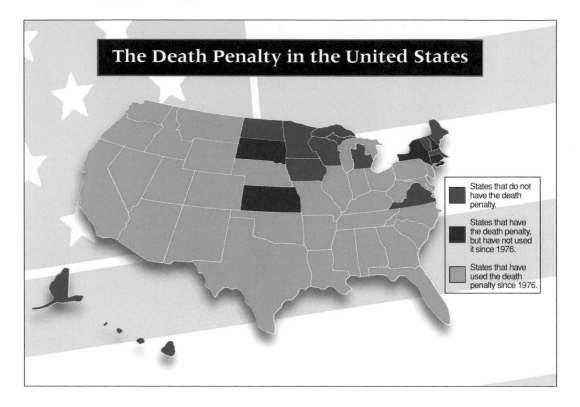

The Death Penalty in the United States

States that do not have the death penalty.

States that have the death penalty, but have not used it since 1976.

States that have used the death penalty since 1976.

Perennial Debates

Much of the debate over the death penalty has remained remarkably constant from debates of years and decades past. One is whether capital punishment deters crime. "The punishment of death," argued writer Samuel Hand in the December 1881 issue of the *North American Review,* "is unquestionably the most powerful deterrent, the most effective preventive, that can be applied." Opponents of the death penalty, on the other hand, have challenged the contention that capital punishment deters murder. Famed defense attorney Clarence Darrow, writing in 1928, argued that "practically all homicides are manifestations of well-recognized human emotions, and it is perfectly plain that fear of excessive punishment does not enter into them. . . . The plea that capital punishment acts as a deterrent to crime will not stand." Arguments over the deterrent value of capital punishment continue to this day.

Another perennial argument is whether capital punishment is morally just. Supporters contend that for some crimes, only death is a punishment justly proportionate to the crime. "In the case of premeditated murder, capital punishment is the only punishment . . . roughly proportionate to the harm that has been done to the murder victim," contends author and lecturer Robert James Bidinotto. But opponents argue that premeditated killing is immoral whether done by individuals or the state. "Allowing our government to kill citizens compromises the deepest moral values upon which this country was conceived: the inviolable dignity of human persons," argues Helen Prejean, a Catholic nun and anti–death penalty activist.

In recent years the perennial debates about the death penalty's morality and effectiveness have been joined by a new concern—that innocent people may be wrongfully executed. Since 1977 more than one hundred death-row inmates have been released from prison after DNA and other new information revealed errors in their trials and convictions. The American Bar Association (ABA) has called for a moratorium on executions "unless and until greater fairness and due process prevail in death penalty implementation."

Effects of the Death Penalty

As the following selections show, much of the ongoing debate over capital punishment in America revolves around its effects on society, and what causal factors affect who receives death sentences. The following selections provide a sampling of the ongoing debate in the United States over the legal and ethical ramifications of the death penalty.

Section One:
Opposing
Viewpoints
on the Death
Penalty

The Death Penalty Should Be Abolished

Bill Kurtis

Bill Kurtis is a television journalist and author of The Death Penalty on Trial: Crisis in American Justice. He describes himself in the following article as a former supporter of the death penalty who now opposes it. Kurtis contends that there are too many errors in death penalty trials and too many innocent people turning up on death row. Such mistakes cannot be accepted when a person's life may be at stake, he concludes.

Consider the following questions:

1. What kinds of mistakes and misconduct led to the faulty conviction of Ray Krone, according to Kurtis?
2. What is "expectational bias" and how can it lead to mistakes, according to Kurtis?
3. How and why did Supreme Court justice Harry Blackmun's views toward capital punishment evolve, according to the author?

We have reached the point in this country where we need to reconsider the death penalty, and morality has nothing to do with it.

There are, quite simply, too many errors in the criminal justice system and too many innocent people turning up on death row. Lawyers have known this for a long time, but it has taken DNA testing to confirm the flaws.

Bill Kurtis, "Is It Time to Rethink the Death Penalty?" *The Newark Star-Ledger*, November 21, 2004. Copyright © 2004 by *The Star-Ledger*. All rights reserved. Reproduced by permission.

How could an innocent defendant be wrongfully convicted in the first place? The answer is mistakes—simple, often tiny, mistakes that can lead to a sentence of death.

Errors and Misconduct

Take the case of Ray Krone, who was arrested for the murder of a bar manager in Phoenix, Ariz., in 1991. An inexperienced forensics expert made a mold of Krone's teeth and placed it around the victim's nipple, hoping to compare the mold with bite marks left by the killer. The mold made contact with the skin and, because a corpse's skin is not resilient, the marks from the mold stayed, creating new evidence from which other experts made their judgments.

Simple mistake. But it became the central piece of evidence that a jury used to convict Krone of murder and sentence him to death. Some 10 years later, DNA tests cleared Krone as a suspect. A sexual offender who lived six blocks away from the victim was the match. He later confessed to the murder.

Investigators might have found the sex offender if they hadn't been directed to build a case against Krone within a few days of the crime. It's a common mistake, focusing too quickly on someone who seems to fit the evidence available. This is called "expectational bias." If the Krone case was a once-only mistake we wouldn't look twice, but DNA's peek through the keyhole of the criminal justice system is telling us such "small mistakes" happen far too often to ignore.

Some errors are not so innocent. A prosecutor learns of an expert witness who does not support his case, and despite his obligation to inform the court about exculpatory evidence he "forgets" to pass it on because it might weaken his case. A jailhouse informant tells the prosecutor what he wants to hear in exchange for lenient treatment. An interrogator uses physical and psychological torture to coerce a confession. An eyewitness confuses media images of the accused or line-up pictures with what she thinks she saw.

Then there's the cozy relationship between police labs and prosecutorial teams—an issue raised by the case of Dennis Williams, who was convicted of a 1978 rape and double murder near Chicago. An Illinois forensic scientist testified that three hairs found in Williams' car matched the hair of the victims. Eight years later, Scotland

Ray Krone, right, accompanied by his lawyer, walks away from prison a free man after spending years on death row for a 1991 murder he did not commit.

Yard examined the hair evidence and said it did not match. Unfortunately, the hair testimony had already sent Williams to death row. He was exonerated in 1996 by DNA testing.

Was it forensic error or forensic fraud? Just when we thought DNA was the ultimate piece of evidence for guilt or innocence, we learn that it can be distorted. Rob Warden, director of the Center on Wrongful Convictions at Northwestern University School of Law reports that "forensic scientists have with disturbing frequency misled juries and sometimes blatantly lied about laboratory results." That's why a defense attorney must always order independent forensic tests. But many of them don't.

Ineffective Counsel

In Illinois, Gov. George Ryan commuted the death sentences of 164 death row inmates to life without parole just before he left office in January 2003. Prosecutors criticized his decision, but Ryan said he acted because Illinois, since 1977, had released more innocent men from death row (13) than it had executed (12). One-third of the 164 inmates, moreover, had been represented by lawyers who had been disbarred or disciplined.

Ineffective counsel is often a problem in death penalty trials. In 1980, for instance, Gary Nelson was charged with killing a 6-year-old girl in Georgia. He was tried, convicted and sentenced to death—all in just two days. His lawyer offered an eight-sentence argument on behalf of his client and was later disbarred.

Likewise, Federico Macias was given the death penalty in 1984 for bludgeoning a couple to death with a machete during a burglary in El Paso, Texas. His court-appointed lawyer was paid $11.84 an hour. The lawyer

Wrongful Convictions

A recent *Chicago Tribune* investigation found that at least 381 homicide convictions across the country have been overturned since 1963 because prosecutors were discovered to have concealed evidence of innocence or because they used evidence they knew to be false.

Progressive, "The Case Against the Death Penalty," February 2000.

failed to call alibi witnesses who would have placed Macias elsewhere during the murders. He failed to cross-examine eyewitnesses. The case was eventually reversed.

Supreme Court Justice Ruth Bader Ginsburg has said: "I have yet to see a death penalty case among the dozens coming to the Supreme Court on eve-of-execution stay applications in which the defendant was well represented. . . . People who are well represented at trial do not get the death penalty."

How many errors occur in death penalty cases? Professor James Liebman of Columbia University School of Law studied 23 years of capital cases and found reversible error in almost seven of every 10 capital sentences, a national average of 68 percent. He concluded in January 2000 that "flaws in America's death-penalty system have reached crisis proportions." Liebman's study

Illinois governor George Ryan commuted the death sentences of all death row inmates in his state.

is not without critics. Prosecutors point out that having a case reversed doesn't mean a defendant is innocent. They argue that it means the system of judicial review is working, ensuring that we won't execute an innocent person.

However, the mistake in Ray Krone's case wasn't caught by an appellate court. There is no guarantee that

Aaron Patterson, right, was one of the death row inmates pardoned by Illinois governor George Ryan in January 2003 because of unsettled questions about his trial.

mistakes inevitably committed in the subtle depths of a trial's tactical decisions or the nuances of testimony and arguments would be caught, either.

A Change of Heart

I used to support the death penalty. But after the Illinois experience, I was shaken by the reality that when DNA testing was applied to the performance of the criminal justice system, 13 inmates on death row were found to be innocent. If we can make that many mistakes, should death hang in the balance?

In the 1976 case *Gregg vs. Georgia,* in which the U.S. Supreme Court allowed state legislatures to reinstate the death penalty if they provided proper guidelines, Justice Thurgood Marshall wrote a dissenting opinion. In it, he said the American people are largely unaware of critical information about the death penalty, saying, " . . . if they were better informed, they would consider it shocking, unjust and unacceptable."

Few people, for instance, are aware that almost no credible study regards the death penalty as a deterrent anymore—or that the average expense of a capital trial is running around $2 million and threatens to bankrupt county budgets in some cases. Similarly, few people know that the quality of justice differs dramatically among the myriad jurisdictions in the United States. The argument against capital punishment grows even stronger when you consider that poor defendants do not get the same quality of defense as wealthy defendants or those defendants whose trials are covered by 24-hour cable networks.

Some states are responding to the warning signs. After Ryan's dramatic action, Illinois enacted more than 80 reforms to ensure that its capital punishment is fair, just and accurate.

I now agree with the American Bar Association that we should abolish the death penalty. And I agree with the late U.S. Supreme Court Justice Harry Blackmun when he wrote, in a dissenting opinion in the 1994 case of *Callins vs. James:* "The basic question—does the system accurately and consistently determine which defendants 'deserve to die'—cannot be answered in the affirmative. . . . The problem is that the inevitability of factual, legal and moral error gives us a system that fails to deliver the fair, consistent, and reliable sentences required by the Constitution."

After a lifetime of upholding the constitutionality of the death penalty, Blackmun withdrew his support, writing, "I feel morally and intellectually obligated simply to concede that the death penalty experiment has failed."

Analyze the essay:

1. Kurtis quotes Supreme Court justice Thurgood Marshall when he states that American public support for the death penalty is caused by ignorance over how capital punishment actually operates in the real world. Does this explain the author's purpose in writing this article?

2. Kurtis argues that having the death penalty creates a risk that innocent people may be executed and cites the story of one individual— Ray Krone—in particular. Does the story of one person provide reason enough to abolish the death penalty?

The Death Penalty Should Be Retained

Paul Rosenzweig

The following viewpoint defending the death penalty focuses on two individuals arrested for a series of sniper attacks that killed several people in the Washington, D.C., area. The author, Paul Rosenzweig, contends that the crimes committed by John Allen Muhammad and Lee Malvo were so heinous that they deserve the death penalty. Abolishing the death penalty has the effect of devaluing the lives of murder victims, the author contends. Rosenzweig also addresses the argument that keeping the death penalty isolates the United States from the rest of the world. He maintains that Americans should not let European views or international organizations control U.S. law. Rosenzweig is a research fellow for the Heritage Foundation and an adjunct law professor at George Mason University.

Consider the following questions:

1. What details does Rosenzweig provide on the sniper victims?
2. How does the death penalty save innocent lives, according to the author?
3. How does Rosenzweig respond to the argument that capital punishment isolates America from other countries that do not have the death penalty?

In October 2002, hundreds of thousands of Washington, D.C.–area residents lived in constant fear of being murdered by mysterious snipers. Eventually, John Allen

Muhammad and Lee Malvo were arrested and charged with 21 cold-blooded, premeditated attacks that killed 14 people across the country—10 of them in the D.C. area alone—and seriously wounded several others. Among the victims:

Convicted sniper John Allen Muhammad, seated next to his attorney, listens to testimony shortly before being sentenced to death on March 9, 2004.

- Lori Ann Lewis-Rivera, 25, mother of a three-year-old. A nanny. Shot while vacuuming her employer's van at a car wash.
- Conrad E. Johnson, 35, bus driver and family man. Father to two sons who cannot understand where their "best friend" went. Killed as he stood on the

steps of his bus waiting to begin his first route of the day.

- Premkumar A. Walekar, 54, father of two, an immigrant from India who came to America in search of an education and a better life. Gunned down as he was filling his taxi with gas.

- Linda Franklin, 47, FBI analyst. Picked off as she loaded bags into her car in a Home Depot parking lot with her husband. She died in his arms.

Malvo and Muhammad allegedly hunted humans like deer, using a high-powered rifle, tripod and scope to drop their prey by shooting through a hole they had drilled in the trunk of their car. Their trials are set to begin this fall [2003]. In jail, young Malvo reportedly has boasted of his feat and laughed about the people he'd executed in cold blood.

The question is, do he and Muhammad deserve a similar fate if convicted?[1]

Some opponents of the death penalty, including many Europeans and other critics of the U.S. say no. They insist that in this day and age, the death penalty is a relic of the past, a barbaric instinct for vengeance no better than the crime it purports to punish.

But such sentiments, however heartfelt, ignore the horrific nature of some criminal deeds. And to do that is, in many senses, to devalue human life itself, for it denies the value of the life of the innocent victim and exalts that of the murderer.

We can see this tendency every time death-penalty opponents object to anyone highlighting the victims. According to opponents, the guilt of their murderers, not the fact that their victims were "good" people, is the central legal issue. But that is precisely backwards. The "legal

---

1. Muhammad was convicted of capital murder on November 17, 2003, and received the death sentence on March 9, 2004. Malvo, who was 17 at the time of his arrest, was convicted of murder in a separate trial and sentenced to life without parole on March 10, 2004, after a jury decided against recommending the death penalty.

issues" are not an end in themselves; they are not what moral philosophers would call an "inherent good." Rather, the legal system is a means to an end—namely, discovering the truth and doing justice. Death-penalty opponents can argue for abolition only by elevating the "system" and devaluing the victim—and calls to ignore the victims show this unfortunate moral calculus at work.

Simply put, there *is* a class of people whose crimes are so heinous, like Malvo and Muhammad, that the death penalty should apply. For those who oppose the death penalty the ultimate thought experiment is: "What would you do with Adolf Hitler?" Anyone who can answer that the principle of non-retribution requires society to permit Hitler to live demonstrates remarkably little regard for any moral calculus that reflects a serious consideration of what it means to be just.

Safeguarding the Innocent

The death penalty is tough on criminals, yes. But any lesser punishment is tougher on *innocent* people. And as a matter of moral justice, do Muhammad and Malvo deserve anything less than execution? Killing should in aggravated cases carry consequences equal to the gravity of the harm caused. People may be free to choose their actions, but in a civilized society, they certainly ought not to be free to choose the *consequences* of those actions. On the contrary, only a barbaric society would permit such behavior to be weakly punished.

Do innocent people ever get caught in the crosshairs of justice? Not as often as death-penalty opponents would have us believe. According to Dudley Sharp, from Justice For All, a nonprofit organization that works on criminal justice reform, "somewhere between 15 and 30 death row inmates have been released from death row with credible evidence of actual innocence. That represents about a 0.3-percent error rate of the 7,300 sentenced to death since 1973." None of these people were

During the 2003 trial of sniper suspect John Allen Muhammad, prosecutor James Willett shows the weapon used in the shootings that killed ten people and terrorized the Washington, D.C., area.

executed before their names were cleared. Those who say otherwise—who think that the error rate is higher—often confuse two types of error. Some cases are reversed because of a legal error about, for example the admissibility of certain evidence: But reversals of this sort are not indicative of the execution of innocents. With respect to that issue—factual errors resulting in the execution of an actually innocent defendant—no case has been identified since the U.S. re-instituted the death penalty in 1973.

Thus, though the risk of error is certainly real, the likelihood of it happening is sufficiently small that we ought not let that small risk that innocents might die prevent us from taking action that would save other innocents.

For that, precisely, is what the death penalty does. It is a deterrent that dissuades people from killing. Indeed, it would be illogical to assume that, as a group, murderers are ignorant of the negative consequences their act could bring. And so it would be equally illogical to assume that some potential murderers are not deterred by the threat of a more severe punishment—namely, execution. Evidence substantiating the deterrent effect of the death penalty is stronger than that against it and supports this intuition. As long ago as 1975 economist Isaac Ehrlich published a study concluding that each additional execution deters seven or eight murders. . . . Without a death penalty you condemn innocents to death at the hands of murderers.

Opponents of the death penalty claim a life sentence is just as harsh a punishment and effective a deterrent as a death sentence for murderers. Not so. Some life sentences come with the possibility of parole. And all sentences short of capital punishment involve the risk that a convicted murderer will escape and prey upon other victims. Furthermore, those who are locked up for life without any possibility of parole have no incentive to refrain from killing fellow inmates and guards. (If they can't possibly be punished any more severely than they already have been, nothing deters them from turning their aggression on others confined with them.) Other convicts sent to prison to serve out sentences, and *not to die* should not be subject to the "death penalty" at the hands of fellow inmates who have no reason to behave.

Why the Oklahoma City Bomber Deserves Execution

We are or ought to be offended by the suggestion that anything less than the death penalty is a suitable punishment for those who commit crimes as monstrous as those of Timothy McVeigh and others like him. He destroyed close to two hundred human lives and all the potential that they might have enjoyed and contributed.

Burton M. Leiser, "Capital Punishment and Retributive Justice," *Free Inquiry,* Summer 2001.

International Criticism

Besides complaining about the unfair nature of the death penalty, American critics also say it isolates us from other countries who oppose it. Despite the overwhelming support for the death penalty among the American public, our continued insistence on it has become a bone of contention with many of our allies, particularly those from Europe, who see it as an antiquated, inhumane policy. It is true that virtually all European nations have abolished the death penalty. The United Nations Commission on Human Rights has, several times over the last few years, drafted resolutions asking nations to impose a moratorium on the death penalty. Many nations around the world already refuse to extradite any criminals to the U.S. that might face the death penalty. Some international

Asay. © by Charles Asay. Reproduced by permission.

Together against the death penalty

Protesters in France rally near a replica of the Statue of Liberty in 2003 to protest America's use of the death penalty.

organizations are even getting involved in U.S. capital punishment cases by filing legal arguments in support of the defendants.

But should we care that some countries object to the death penalty and thus are turning up the pressure on the U.S. to abandon the practice? No. European views shouldn't control American law. . . .

Why does the European Union reject the notion of requiring a murderer to give his life as penance for his crime? At the heart of their outrage are, they claim, civil rights concerns. They say that every human being has a fundamental right to life. True. But the European Union and its abolitionist allies never turn the challenge around and ask: What of the right to life of the murdered? The rights of the victims and their families? If we refuse to punish those who kill, then where do those pained by their crimes turn for justice? More prosaically, though execution is physically identical to murder, it is both morally and legally distinct—a distinction that the abolitionist view simply ignores.

Death is different—it requires different legal mechanisms and a different moral calculus. For this reason we must be cautious in imposing it and America has developed a complex (some would say too complex) series of mechanisms to insure accuracy. But caution does not require inaction. Those outside America who oppose capital punishment urge, in effect, moral equivalency between murderer and victim. Worse yet, if our concept of deterrence is anywhere close to accurate, they condemn countless unnamed and never-to-be-identified victims to acts of violence that might have been deterred.

Or, to return to where we began: the argument for the death penalty can be restated in two words: Lee Malvo.

And if you need two more, think of victim Linda Franklin.

Analyze the essay:

1. Rosenzweig focuses on John Allen Muhammad and Lee Malvo and their victims. Why might he want the reader to focus on the victims of crime? What effect did Muhammad and Malvo's actions have on the victims? What would be the effect of sparing the lives of the two killers, according to the author?

2. Rosenzweig argues that abolishing the death penalty would have a harmful moral effect of depriving criminals of their just punishment. What arguments does he make to back this contention? How would abolishing the death penalty harm innocent people?

The Death Penalty Prevents Murder

Jeff Jacoby

Much of the death penalty debate turns on the question of what effect capital punishment has on the behavior of criminals. Death penalty supporters contend that criminals who might kill their victims do not do so because of the fear of being executed. In this essay, syndicated columnist Jeff Jacoby makes this argument by examining a time in American history when the death penalty was seldom used, and notes that the number of murders during that period greatly increased. He goes on to argue that since executions have become more numerous in recent years, the number of murders has declined. Jacoby concludes by arguing that capital punishment saves innocent lives.

Consider the following questions:

1. Does Jacoby provide any reasons for why a death penalty moratorium could have caused increased murder rates?
2. What implications does the author draw from the murder rate in Texas?
3. How does Jacoby respond to the argument that capital punishment should be stopped because America's criminal justice system is flawed?

Death penalty abolitionists don't usually mention it, but in promoting a moratorium on executions, they are urging us down a road we have taken before.

In the mid-1960s, as a number of legal challenges to capital punishment began working their way through the courts, executions in the United States came to a halt. From 56 in 1960, the number of killers put to death dropped to seven in 1965, to one in 1966, and to zero in 1967. There it stayed for the next 10 years, until the State of Utah executed Gary Gilmore in 1977. That was the only execution in 1977, and there were only two more during the next three years.

In sum, between 1965 and 1980, there was practically no death penalty in the United States, and for 10 of those 16 years—1967–76—there was *literally* no death penalty: a national moratorium.

The Effects of No Death Penalty

What was the effect of making capital punishment unavailable for a decade and a half? Did a moratorium on executions save innocent lives—or cost them?

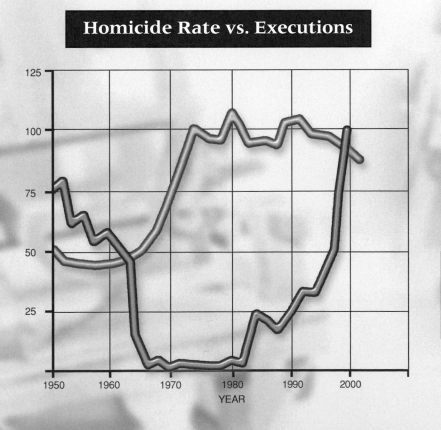

Homicide Rate vs. Executions

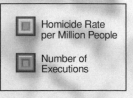

Homicide Rate per Million People

Number of Executions

Source: Death Penalty Information Center, National Center for Health Statistics.

The data are brutal. Between 1965 and 1980, annual murders in the United States skyrocketed, rising from 9,960 to 23,040. The murder rate—homicides per 100,000 persons—doubled from 5.1 to 10.2.

Was it just a fluke that the steepest increase in murder in US history coincided with the years when the death penalty was not available to punish it? Perhaps. Or perhaps murder becomes more attractive when potential killers know that prison is the worst outcome they can face.

By contrast, common sense suggests that there are at least some people who will *not* commit murder if they think it might cost them their lives. Sure enough, as executions have become more numerous, murder has declined. "From 1995 to 2000," notes Dudley Sharp of the victims rights group Justice For All, "executions averaged 71 per year, a 21,000 percent increase over the 1966–1980 period. The

A jury's decision to sentence convicted murderer Scott Peterson to death in December 2004 makes newspaper headlines.

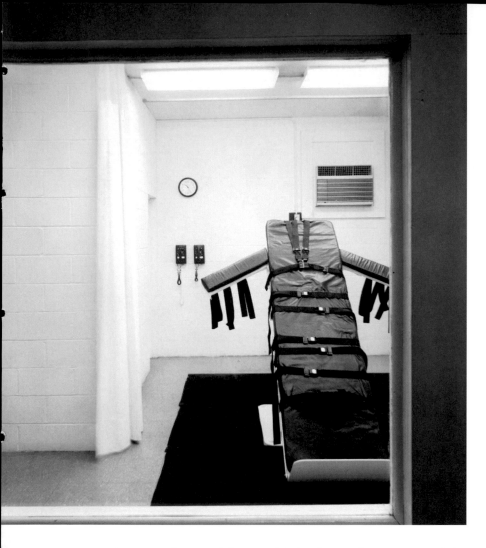

A lethal injection chamber. Lethal injection is the most common method of execution in the United States today.

murder rate dropped from a high of 10.2 (per 100,000) in 1980 to 5.7 in 1999—a 44 percent reduction. The murder rate is now at its lowest level since 1966."

What is true nationally has been observed locally as well. There were 12,652 homicides in New York during the 25 years from 1940 to 1965, when New York regularly executed murderers. By contrast, during the 25 years from 1966 to 1991 there were no executions at all—and murders quadrupled to 51,638.

To be sure, murder rates fell in almost every state in the 1990s. But they fell the most in states that use capital punishment. The most striking protection of innocent life has been in Texas, which executes more murderers

Pro–death penalty demonstrators supported the decision to execute Oklahoma City bomber Timothy McVeigh.

than any other state. In 1991, the Texas murder rate was 15.3 per 100,000. By 1999, it had fallen to 6.1—a drop of 60 percent. Within Texas, the most aggressive death penalty prosecutions are in Harris County (the Houston area). Since the resumption of executions in 1982, the annual number of Harris County murders has plummeted from 701 to 241—a 72 percent decrease.

Obviously, murder and the rate at which it occurs are affected by more than just the presence or absence of the death penalty. But even after taking that caveat into account, it seems irrefutably clear that when murderers are executed, innocent lives are saved. And when executions are stopped, innocent lives are lost.

Death penalty abolitionists (and a few death penalty supporters) claim that a moratorium on executions is warranted because the criminal justice system is "broken" and the death penalty is unfairly applied. But if that's true when the punishment is death, how much more so is it true when the punishment isn't death! Death penalty prosecutions typically undergo years of appeals, often attracting intense scrutiny and media attention. So painstaking is the super-due process of capital murder cases that for all the recent hype about innocent prisoners on death row, there is not a single proven case in modern times of an innocent person being executed in the United States.

Abolishing Prisons?

But the due process in non–death penalty cases is not nearly as scrupulous. Everyone knows that there are innocent people behind bars today. If the legal system's flaws justify a moratorium on capital punishment, a *fortiori* [with more reason], they justify a moratorium on imprisonment. Those who call for a moratorium on executions should be calling just as vehemently for a moratorium on prison terms. Why don't they?

> ## The Death Penalty's Deterrence Effect
>
> Three major studies were released in 2001, all finding for the deterrent effect of the death penalty. One . . . out of the University of Houston, found that a temporary halt to executions in Texas resulted in an additional 90–150 murders, because of the reduction in deterrence.
>
> Dudley Sharp, "Do We Need the Death Penalty? It Is Just and Right," *World & I*, September 2002.

Because they know how ridiculous it would sound. If there are problems with the system, the system should be fixed, but refusing to punish criminals would succeed only in making society far less safe than it is today.

The same would be true of a moratorium on executions. If due process in capital murder cases can be made even more watertight, by all means let us do so. But not by keeping the worst of our murderers alive until perfection is achieved. We've been down the moratorium road before. We know how that experiment turns out. The results are written in wrenching detail on gravestones across the land.

Analyze the essay:

1. Jacoby says that the correlation between the moratorium on executions and an increase in the murder rate was either "just a fluke" or due to the fact that capital punishment deters murder. How does framing the choice this way help support his favorable opinion of the death penalty?

2. Some death penalty opponents argue that because a flawed criminal justice system sometimes convicts innocent people, capital punishment should be abolished. What would be the effects of applying this logic not just for capital cases, but for all criminal cases, according to Jacoby? What does he conclude from his logical exercise?

The Death Penalty Increases Murder

Frederick C. Millett

In the following essay Frederick C. Millett describes several effects of capital punishment—results that he believes serve to demonstrate the death penalty's impracticality in fighting murder and crime. One effect is the money communities spend to try capital cases and administer the death penalty—money that he believes could otherwise be spent on more police or other crime-fighting resources. Millett also disputes the claim that capital punishment decreases murder by deterring criminals, arguing instead that capital punishment may have the opposite effect of increasing the number of murders committed. Millett is a law student and the creator of the End the Death Penalty Now! Web site.

Consider the following questions:
1. With his opening sentences, what does Millett say he intends to achieve with his essay?
2. How does Millett use comparative statistics between homicide rates and capital punishment in different parts of the country?
3. What reasons does the author provide in arguing that capital punishment does not deter people from committing homicides?

In this essay I will try to prove that even if one believes that the death penalty is morally acceptable, it should still be abolished based on practical reasons. The death penalty serves no purpose in our society anymore. It now

Frederick C. Millett, "Part II: Practical Reasons," End the Death Penalty Now! www.msu. edu/~millettf/DeathPenalty, December 3, 2004. Copyright © 2004 by Frederick C. Millett. Reproduced by permission.

costs more money to sentence someone to death than to imprison them for life and, contrary to popular belief, the death penalty does not deter murders from occurring. . . .

The Truth About Death Penalty Costs

There have been hundreds of studies done concerning the cost of the death penalty—and not one of them proves that the death sentence saves money. In a study done in North Carolina, the death penalty costs them $2.16 million more than a sentence of life imprisonment without parole. In Texas, the death penalty costs around $2.3 million, nearly three times the cost of imprisoning someone in a maximum security jail for forty years. Yet Texas still has one of the highest murder rates in the country. Where does all this money come from? The DPIC [Death Penalty Information Center, a nonprofit organization that opposes capital punishment and provides analysis and information on death penalty issues] has the answer, which should really upset most people:

> Across the country, police are being laid off, prisoners are being released early, the courts are clogged, and crime continues to rise. The economic recession has caused cutbacks in the backbone of the criminal justice system. In Florida, the budget crisis resulted in the early release of 3,000 prisoners. In Texas, prisoners are serving only 20% of their time and rearrests are common. Georgia is laying off 900 correctional personnel and New Jersey has had to dismiss 500 police officers. Yet these same states, and many others like them, are pouring millions of dollars into the death penalty with no resultant reduction in crime.

The death penalty is causing government officials to lose jobs, and most importantly, police to be removed from the streets. How can we stop crime if we do not have more police in the area? New Jersey had to dismiss 500 police officers to pay for death penalty costs, yet politicians are still praising the death penalty as a great way to fight crime. The numbers just don't add up. The death penalty is in fact making America a more unsafe place to live, because funds are going to the death penalty instead of more needed crime-fighting strategies. . . .

In California, the death penalty costs $90 million annually over what it would cost for an ordinary murder trial. $78 million of that money is spent on the trial level alone, proving that the majority of death penalty costs come

A death penalty opponent expresses her belief that money spent on capital punishment could be better used for health care, education, and other areas.

from the trial level—not the appeals process like everyone thinks. The DPIC says the following about death penalty costs:

> The death penalty is much more expensive than its closest alternative—life imprisonment with no parole. Capital trials are longer and more expensive at every step than other murder trials. Pre-trial motions, expert witness investigations, jury selection and the necessity for two trials—one on guilt and one on sentencing—make capital cases extremely costly, even before the appeals process begins. Guilty pleas are almost unheard of when the punishment is death. In addition, many of these trials result in a life sentence rather than the death penalty, so the state pays the cost of life imprisonment on top of the expensive trial.

The death penalty is a very costly, very useless activity. It is definitely more practical to use an alternative to the death penalty, which will save taxpayers millions of dollars and put more police on the streets. With the amount of money saved, crime-fighting programs could be put to the test and government spending could be put to a better use. Now is as good a time as ever for this nation to realize its faults and eliminate the death penalty.

Deterrence Effect

Hundreds of studies have also been done concerning the deterrence effect of capital punishment. The fact is, the death penalty does not deter murders from occurring. In one study done in Oklahoma, it was found that after Oklahoma resumed capital punishment, no deterrent effect was found—in fact, a brutalization effect (increase in homicides) was reported. This means that capital punishment doesn't lower crime rates, but in fact raises them. William Bailey, author of the report in Oklahoma, also found a significant increase in stranger-related deaths

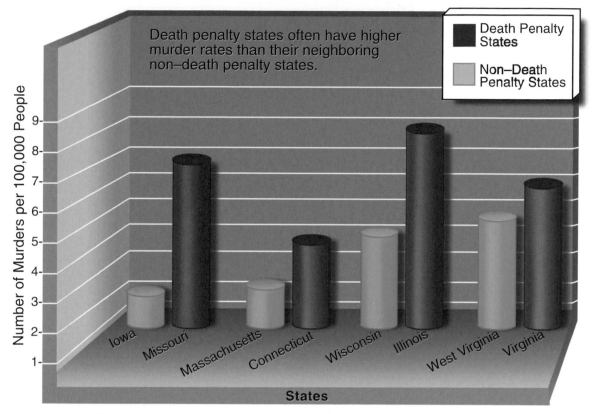

Does the Death Penalty Deter Crime?

Death penalty states often have higher murder rates than their neighboring non–death penalty states.

Legend: Death Penalty States / Non–Death Penalty States

Number of Murders per 100,000 People

States: Iowa, Missouri, Massachusetts, Connecticut, Wisconsin, Illinois, West Virginia, Virginia

Source: Death Penalty Information Center, www.deathpenaltyinfo.org.

after Oklahoma resumed the death penalty. In other reports in Texas and California, the same information was reported—proving that the death penalty almost never has a deterrent effect on crime.

Another way to prove that capital punishment does not deter homicides is to look at homicide rates throughout the country. In 2000, the South once again had the highest homicide rate in the nation, at 6.8 murders per 100,000. The South also executes more than a majority of death row inmates, comprising 80% of the nation's executions (90% in 2000). The Northeast, on the other hand, had the lowest homicide rate, and comprises less

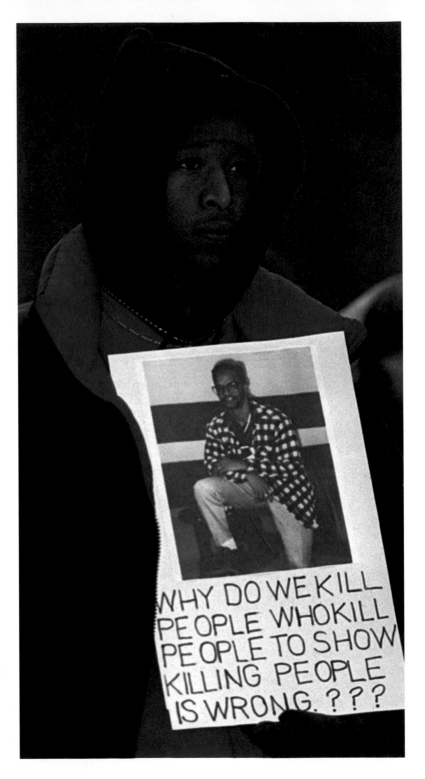

For some, the death penalty is a personal issue. Here, Dontae Taylor protests the death sentence imposed on his uncle.

than 1% of the nation's executions. Comparing states without the death penalty to states with the death penalty, you will also find higher homicide rates for the latter. States without the death penalty have an average homicide rate of 3.6, compared to 5.5 for states with the death penalty (per 100,000). And finally, when looking at neighboring states, with one with and one without the death penalty, statistics have shown that the state without the death penalty has lower homicide rates. . . .

Police are aware of this fact as well. A 1995 poll of police chiefs showed that the police do not believe that the death penalty lowers homicide rates. . . .

All these previous statements make sense when you think reasonably about the death penalty. First of all, the death penalty costs millions of dollars more than life imprisonment, causing a decrease of police officers on the streets and a decrease in regular jail time for criminals with lesser offenses. With less police and more criminals on the streets, it is obvious that crime and homicide rates will go up.

Also, the death penalty has the opposite effect, in my opinion, on a civilized society. Because the government finds it all right to kill, others could see it all right as well. The government needs to set a good example, telling people that any kind of killing, even state-sanctioned murder, is wrong. How can we be so hypocritical by saying that killing is wrong, but if it's done by the state to a criminal, it's all right? This is setting a bad example for the people in this country. It's no wonder that homicide rates go up after an execution—someone hears that the state has killed someone so they feel like they can go out and kill someone too.

The Death Penalty's Effect in Oklahoma

Oklahoma's return to capital punishment in 1990 was followed by a significant increase in killings that involved strangers, with an increase of one stranger homicide per month for the year following an execution.

Gary W. Potter, statement before the Joint Interim Health and Welfare Committee, Kentucky Legislature, March 20, 1999.

Another obvious explanation to these statistics is seen when we look at why people commit homicides. Murderers never think about being caught in the first place, so why should they be frightened by the death penalty? As well, crimes of passion comprise a large percent of homicides in this country. During these murders, the killer is not thinking straight and is feeding off emotions. The last thing they'd think about is punishment.

I hope I have proven that capital punishment is not a practical solution to crime in the United States. By using this method, we are taking police off the streets and because of lack of funds, allowing criminals to be paroled with only a short time in jail. This is causing America to be a more dangerous, and expensive, place to live in—a place where justice is not served.

Analyze the essay:

1. Millett makes extensive use of information from the Death Penalty Information Center, an organization that opposes the death penalty. Does his reliance on this source weaken his position, in your view? Why or why not?
2. How similar are the first and last paragraphs of Millett's essay? Does stating and restating his arguments help tie the essay together, or do they seem too repetitive?

The Death Penalty Helps Relatives of Murder Victims

Gail B. Stewart

Family members of murder victims have played an active role in the debate over capital punishment. Relatives often testify before juries who are deciding whether to put convicted criminals to death. In some states family members are allowed to personally witness the execution of their relative's killer. In the following essay writer Gail B. Stewart examines how families are affected by violent crime and by capital punishment. She presents the view that the death penalty can bring peace of mind and serve as an important step toward recovery for grieving families. Stewart is the author of more than eighty books for young adults.

Consider the following questions:

1. What stories does Stewart tell of how Andy Serpico and Vicki Haack were affected by the criminal justice system following the murder of family members?
2. What distinction does the author make between "vengeance" and "retribution"?

When Bonnie Serpico was raped and murdered in 1979, her husband, Andy, was outraged by the way the trial and clemency hearings of her assailant, James Free, were handled by the justice system. He was not allowed to mention to the jury that he and his wife had children—the judge felt it would be prejudicial to the jury. He and his daughters weren't even allowed to sit where the jury could get a good look at them, whereas James Free's mother was allowed to sit right in front of the jury.

The emphasis, fumed Serpico, was not on the victim, and the cruel way she had been killed. Instead, the focus was on the killer. Said Serpico, "Everybody would get to meet James Free, get to know James Free. I wanted people to remember that Bonnie Serpico was a real person."

Oklahoma City bombing survivor Sue Ashford was one of ten people selected by lottery to witness the execution of convicted bomber Timothy McVeigh on June 11, 2001.

But in recent years there has been a move toward recognizing the rights of crime victims and their families. It is increasingly common for a tearful family member to address the convicted murderer in court, to be given an opportunity to express the grief and pain resulting from the loss of a wife, a husband, a brother, a daughter. And sixteen states allow victims' families to view executions, the idea being that the victim's loved ones can gain peace of mind through the killer's death.

"We've been trying to sensitize people to the fact that victims should not be considered outsiders in the criminal justice system," explains one activist for victims' rights. "They have a stake; they should be in the forefront. We deserve and demand a place at the table."

Some might argue that such, "peace of mind" and having "a place at the table" are merely euphemisms for vengeance—hardly a civilized response in our modern society. However, "vengeance" is not an accurate word; retribution is what society hungers for, at a time when the United States seems to be awash in violent crime. It is not vengeance that victims' families seek—that would be almost impossible. . . .

Indeed, many protest that if they were out only for vengeance, they would be disappointed, for no form of execution today can match the savagery of what murder victims go through. How, for example, can death by lethal injection "equal" the death by raping and strangulation, or the torture of mutilation? Or multiple murder?

No, it isn't merely vengeance, but retribution—a way that society can balance the scales, says Jack Collins, whose daughter was brutally raped, beaten, tortured, and murdered:

> It's a way of giving the victims and their families a feeling of satisfaction for what was done to them, to make them whole as far as possible or restore integrity—the quality or state of completeness—to both the people and the system. Nothing will ever bring Suzanne

back to us. But even if this retribution doesn't bring complete closure, it shows us that society, the jury, and the entire criminal justice system care enough about us to see to it that our daughter's killer receives his appropriate punishment. It lets us know that they did right by us as far as they could.

The execution of a killer, while certainly not single-handedly healing the wounds for victims, can certainly be an important step in the process, as Vicki Haack and her family learned recently. In 1986 a crack addict named Kenneth Harris had entered Haack's sister's apartment, raped and choked her, and then spent almost an hour drowning her in the bathtub.

In June 1997, Haack and her family stood in a small viewing room as Harris was strapped to a gurney in the Huntsville, Texas, penitentiary. Haack had rid herself of her rage and hatred of Harris, she says, but she still was in favor of Harris's execution. "We have no hate or bitterness in our hearts," she explains, "but that doesn't mean he does not pay for his crime." The payment, says Haack, was exacted by the state; however, in the moments before he was injected with the lethal chemicals that would kill him, Harris turned to Haack and her family and said, "I hope you can go on with your lives and we can put an end to this."

Devaluing Life

What happens when the punishment goes unserved, or when it is far less severe than the crime? To put a murderer behind bars for a decade or so, a punishment that is effectively the same as an embezzler would get, is disrespectful. It devalues the life that was lost, making a mockery of justice.

Jay and Shari Sawyer react after witnessing the execution of Timothy McVeigh on closed-circuit television. Shari's mother was one of McVeigh's 168 victims.

Donnetta Apple's brother was killed in the bombing of the Murrah federal building in Oklahoma City. Although never a supporter of the death penalty, Apple feels now that anything less than death would be a slap in the face to her brother and the 167 others who were killed in the bombing. To her, she says, it boils down to the concept of making choices—one of the most important, basic parts of life:

> [Timothy McVeigh] chose to park that truck, put in his earplugs, and walk off. When he did that, he took away the rights of 168 people to ever make decisions of their own again. My brother and the others can't elect to work, or play, or spend time with their families. So I don't want McVeigh to have the freedom to even get a drink of water in his cell. If those 168 victims can't make the most basic of choices, why should he? [He] has to pay for the choice he made on April 19, 1995—and he has to pay with his life.

It is time we paid attention to the victims of the unspeakable crimes that occur in our society. They—more than anyone—understand the pain and loss that such crimes cause. They deserve the healing and closure that can come with resolution. And their voices need to be heard.

Analyze the essay:

1. How does having victims tell their own stories of how they were personally affected help support the argument that the death penalty has helped them?
2. How does not killing murderers affect innocent bystanders, according to Stewart? What examples does she provide to support her argument?

The Death Penalty Hurts Relatives of Murder Victims

Pat Bane

Pat Bane, the author of the following viewpoint, lost an uncle to a violent mugging but remained a lifelong opponent of the death penalty. In the following essay she argues that family members are profoundly affected by crime, but that the death penalty does not provide peace of mind and closure to them. It instead often traumatizes them and prevents them from dealing with their grief, she writes. Bane is executive director of Murder Victims' Families for Reconciliation (MVFR), a national organization of families who have lost loved ones to violent crime and who oppose capital punishment.

Consider the following questions:

1. What are the two main issues families who have lost loved ones to crime must deal with, according to Bane?
2. Why do families of victims feel cheated after executions, in Bane's view?

The death penalty is not a solution to violence. It is a premeditated act of violence carried out on behalf of us all. Since reinstatement of the death penalty in the U.S. in 1976, executions in Virginia have been steadily increasing. Today, the state ranks behind only Texas and Florida in the number of its citizens executed. Historically, it was the first colony to perform an execution and has killed more people, including women and children, than any other state.

Pat Bane, "Seeking Alternatives to the Death Penalty," *The Virginian Pilot*, October 30, 1996. Copyright © 1996 by Landmark Communications, Inc. Reproduced by permission.

A 1995 Hart Research poll showed that police chiefs across the country do not believe that the death penalty is effective in reducing violent crime. It is irreversible when errors are discovered, is more costly than life sentencing, and simply does not accomplish what society expects it will. Still, legislators in Virginia and 37 other states try to appear tough on crime by supporting capital punish-

Death penalty trials and hearings can be emotionally trying for relatives and close associates of the murder victim.

ment. More and more, we hear that the death penalty provides closure to families of murder victims. There has even been legislation passed allowing victims' families to witness executions.

From Sept. 21 to Oct. 6 [1996], members of Murder Victims' Families for Reconciliation (MVFR), this national organization of families who have lost a loved one to homicide or state execution, came from across the U.S., Canada and Ireland to join members in Virginia to advocate alternatives to the death penalty. They spoke of personal losses and reasons for rejecting the death penalty to over 25,000 people at 225 events during a 16-day public education tour called the Journey of Hope.

When a family loses a loved one to murder, it has two major issues to deal with. One is a crime. The other is a

Cathy Wilburn lost two grandsons in the Oklahoma City bombing, but later stated she would get "no relief" from convicted bomber Timothy McVeigh's execution.

death and the grief that accompanies such loss. The first contacts a family has after a murder are with law enforcement officers and prosecutors. It is not the police agencies' or district attorney's job to assist families in dealing with grief. So, in shock and through these legal contacts, family members usually become focused on the crime. By seeking an execution at this time of crisis, society implies to victim's families that they will feel better when the offender is killed.

Nancy Gowen, a Richmond woman whose mother was murdered, told audiences that the subsequent execution only added to the horror. Families who oppose the death penalty, rather than being comforted, are further traumatized by an execution being carried out in their names. Those who expect an execution to bring release from unresolved rage and emptiness often complain that the execution was too easy, that the murderer did not suffer enough. Many feel cheated when the execution does not provide the anticipated relief.

Are we really so lacking in sensitivity and compassion that we believe killing heals? Do we truly think those who have lost a child, parent, spouse, sibling or other family member will find solace in the death of another human being? The all too tragic truth is that nothing—no number of retaliatory deaths—can ever restore the lives lost. Society can provide support and grief therapy to families of murder victims. Churches and social-service agencies can offer hope by reaching out to grieving families enabling them to heal. MVFR families have found that dealing with their grief rather than seeking retaliation has enabled them to go on living.

Politicians who offer victims' families only another death and the gruesome specter of watching someone die must provide real solutions. Communities should no longer accept ineffective and expensive policies that fail to make our streets safe. Our representatives must be held accountable to provide programs that prevent crime. Their current emphasis on execution brutalizes us all while accomplishing nothing.

Analyze the essay:
1. What are the major effects that violent crime has on families, and how are these effects made worse by use of the death penalty, according to Bane? What are the harms of false hopes?
2. How does Bane use rhetorical questions in her second-to-last paragraph to question the positive effects of witnessing executions? What answer to these questions is implied?

The Death Penalty Is Inhumane

Robert Murray

Many states have adopted the lethal injection method of execution because it is believed to be more humane than previous methods such as electrocution or the gas chamber. In the following viewpoint Robert Murray argues that a humane method of execution is a fantasy. Capital punishment creates intense anxiety and psychological torment for people on death row regardless of the method of execution. Murray writes from personal experience. In 1992 he was sentenced to death, along with his brother, for two murders committed in 1991. He remains imprisoned in Arizona pending legal appeals. He has since written the book *Life on Death Row*.

Consider the following questions:

1. What factors caused the state of Arizona to replace the gas chamber with lethal injection, according to Murray?
2. What analogy does the author use to describe death by injection?

The gas chamber was introduced to Arizona in the 1930s. Before that, the state hanged people. Nooses from every execution were saved and displayed in glass cases on the walls of the witness chamber of the death house. Hanging was discontinued after a woman was accidentally decapitated in 1930.

Robert Murray, "It's Not Like Falling Asleep," *Harper's Magazine*, vol. 301, November 2000, p. 15. Copyright © 2000 by *Harper's Magazine*. Reproduced by permission of the author.

On April 6, 1992, at 12:18 A.M., Donald Harding was pronounced dead after spending a full eleven minutes in the state's gas chamber. It was Arizona's first execution in twenty-nine years, and state officials were somewhat out of practice. The spectacle of Harding gasping in the execution chamber was a little too hard for people to handle. In response, a movement grew to make executions more "humane."

Suddenly there was a new political crisis. People were outraged. Politicians took to the stump. State execution was cruel, ghastly, horrid. It took a prisoner eleven minutes to cough up his life to the gas. Of course, if executions could be made to seem more humane, that was something else altogether.

Protesters demonstrate outside California State Prison at San Quentin. California gives people sentenced to death a choice between the gas chamber and lethal injection.

It was a wonderful political banner to wave come election time: Arizona would continue to execute people, but they would be nice executions. The politicians went about their task with glee. They preserved their right to kill people by coming up with a new way to kill people. Lethal injection was their new champion, and champion it they did.

A museum exhibit in Texas features the tools used in the lethal injection executions of two convicted murderers.

Seven months after Harding's execution, a new law was born: "Any person sentenced to death prior to November 23, 1992, is afforded a choice of execution by either lethal gas or lethal injection. Inmates receiving death after November 23, 1992, are to be executed by lethal injection."

As it happened, my brother Roger and I were sentenced to death on October 26, 1992. We were among the lucky few who were given a . . . choice about how we should die.

Offering prisoners a "humane" execution seems to be the latest strategy to keep capital punishment alive. But the notion that any execution could be humane eludes me. People today seem generally happy with the idea of lethal injection, as long as it is done in a neat, sanitary, easy-to-watch fashion. I'm not sure what this says about our society. However, I am sure most people don't grasp the reality of the "sleeping" death of which they so widely approve. Indeed, many witnesses leave an execution with a serene look on their faces, as if they'd just seen a somewhat pleasant movie. To my mind, it's actually the witnesses who are falling asleep at injection killings, lulled by the calmness of it all.

The Airplane Analogy

As I see it, death by injection is very like being tossed out of an airplane. Suppose I'm told that on November 3, someone will escort me from my cell, take me up in an airplane, and, at three o'clock in the afternoon, toss me out without a parachute. After a few minutes, my body will hit a target area, killing me immediately. It's an easy, instant, painless death. The impact of hitting the ground after falling several thousand feet will kill me as instantly and effectively as lethal injection.

Killing inmates by tossing them out of airplanes would of course be unacceptable to the public. But why? It's as fast and effective as lethal injection. The terror of falling two minutes isn't all that different from the terror of lying

Sargent. © 2000 by Universal Press Syndicate. Reproduced by permission.

strapped to a table; and neither is physically painful. There's a similar waiting process before each execution. If an airplane is used, you wait for the time it takes the aircraft to take off and reach the target area at the proper altitude. For lethal injection, you wait in the death house until everything's ready and all possibility of a stay of execution has been exhausted. In an airplane, a cargo door is opened: in the death house, a curtain across the viewing window is drawn back. In an airplane, you are thrown to an absolute death and witnesses watch your body fall. In the death house, you are strapped to a gurney and witnesses watch state officials inject you with sodium pentothal. In both cases, death is sudden and final.

To me they are the same. I will feel the same powerful emotions and chaotic anxiety either way. But the public would never describe my death by falling from an aircraft as "simply falling asleep." They would be outraged.

Politicians would rush to give speeches about giving prisoners a "choice," and the law would be changed.

The public would cry out, not because the prisoner died an agonizing and painful death but because most people feel that the anxiety of being tossed from an aircraft without a parachute would be too terrible for an inmate to bear, and the spectacle of death would be too terrible for observers to bear. In this case, the public would be forced to understand the emotions an inmate feels before execution; when lethal injection is used, all such emotions are hidden behind a veil that is not drawn aside until the moment before death.

This airplane analogy is as close as I can come to illustrating the fallacy of the humane execution. There is much more to death by injection than just falling asleep, beginning with the long wait on death row (where execution is a constant presence), the terror of being taken to the death house, the helpless panic of being strapped to a table, and finally the sense of utter loss as the curtain is opened. All of the fear and anxiety of falling from an aircraft is present when the injection begins. Both are horrible by any measure. And neither is anything like falling asleep.

Analyze the essay:

1. The author speaks from personal experience as a death row prisoner. Does his status make his speculative part of what death by injection would feel like more or less convincing, in your view?

2. What would be the effect on public opinion if states chose to execute people by tossing them out of airplanes? What point is the author trying to make about the public's views about capital punishment?

Sparing Murderers the Death Penalty Is Inhumane

Wesley Lowe

Wesley Lowe is a writer of fantasy novels and the creator of the Pro Death Penalty Webpage, from which the following selection is taken. He argues that replacing the death penalty with life imprisonment would have negative consequences for many because people cannot rely on the criminal justice system to carry out lifetime sentences. He recounts the stories of two convicted murderers who were spared the death penalty, including one who was released from prison and killed several women in Texas.

Consider the following questions:

1. What assumption does Lowe make about the parents of Pamela Ross and their reaction to the fact that their daughter's killer is eligible for parole?
2. What is the average prison sentence served for murder, according to the author?

Abolitionists claim that there are alternatives to the death penalty. They say that life in prison without parole serves just as well. Certainly, if you ignore all the murders criminals commit within prison when they kill prison guards and other inmates, and also when they kill decent citizens upon escape. . . .

Wesley Lowe, "Capital Punishment vs. Life Without Parole," Pro Death Penalty Webpage, www.wesleylowe.com/cp.html, January 25, 2005. Copyright © 2005 by Wesley Lowe. Reproduced by permission.

The Moss Case

Another flaw is that life imprisonment tends to deteriorate with the passing of time. Take the Moore case in New York State for example.

In 1962, James Moore raped and strangled 14-year-old Pamela Moss. Her parents decided to spare Moore the death penalty on the condition that he be sentenced to life in prison without parole. Later on, thanks to a change in sentencing laws in 1982, James Moore is eligible for parole every two years!

If Pamela's parents knew that they couldn't trust the state, Moore could have been executed long ago and they could have put the whole horrible incident behind them

Death penalty proponents celebrate outside California's San Quentin prison following the midnight execution of convicted murderer Keith Daniel Williams on May 3, 1996.

forever. Instead they have a nightmare to deal with bian-nually. I'll bet not a day goes by that they don't kick themselves for being foolish enough to trust the liberal sham that is life imprisonment and rehabilitation. (According to the U.S. Department of Justice, the average prison sentence served for murder is five years and eleven months.)

Putting a murderer away for life just isn't good enough. Laws change, so do parole boards, and people forget the past. Those are things that cause life imprisonment to weather away. As long as the murderer lives, there is always a chance, no matter how small, that he will strike again. And there are people who run the criminal justice system who are naive enough to allow him to repeat his crime.

Kenneth McDuff

Kenneth McDuff, for instance, was convicted of the 1966 shooting deaths of two boys and the vicious rape-strangulation of their 16-year-old female companion. A Fort Worth jury ruled that McDuff should die in the electric chair, a sentence commuted to life in prison in 1972 after the U.S. Supreme Court struck down the death penalty as then imposed. In 1989, with Texas prisons overflowing and state officials under fire from the federal judiciary, McDuff was quietly turned loose on an unsuspecting citizenry.

Within days, a naked body of a woman turned up. Prostitute Sarafia Parker, 31, had been beaten, strangled and dumped in a field near Temple. McDuff's freedom in 1989 was interrupted briefly. Jailed after a minor racial incident, he slithered through the system and was out again in 1990.

In early 1991, McDuff enrolled at Texas State Technical College in Waco. Soon, Central Texas prostitutes began

> ## Prisoners Who Murder Again
>
> In 1994, an inmate who already was serving two life sentences in the Philadelphia Industrial Correctional Center was sentenced to three more after he was convicted of stabbing three prison guards. . . . The fact is that murderers who already are imprisoned murder again.
>
> Michael Tremoglie, "Capital Punishment Canards," *Insight on the News*, March 4, 2003.

Convicted murderer Kenneth McDuff was released from prison in 1989. He killed several more people before being arrested and convicted again.

Wright. © 2003 by Cagle Cartoons. Reproduced by permission.

disappearing. One, Valencia Joshua, 22, was last seen alive Feb. 24, 1991. Her naked, decomposed body later was discovered in a shallow grave in woods behind the college. Another of the missing women, Regenia Moore, was last seen kicking and screaming in the cab of McDuff's pickup truck. During the Christmas holidays of 1991, Colleen Reed disappeared from an Austin car wash. Witnesses reported hearing a woman scream that night and seeing two men speeding away in a yellow or tan Thunderbird. Little more than two months later, on March 1, 1992, Melissa Northrup, pregnant with a third child, vanished from the Waco convenience store where she worked. McDuff's beige Thunderbird, broken down, was discovered a block from the store.

Fifty-seven days later, a fisherman found the young woman's nearly nude body floating in a gravel pit in Dallas County, 90 miles north of Waco. By then, McDuff was the target of a nationwide manhunt. Just days after Mrs. Northrup's funeral, McDuff was recognized on television's "America's Most Wanted" and arrested May 4 in Kansas City.

In 1993, a Houston jury ordered him executed for the kidnap-slaying of 22-year-old Melissa Northrup, a Waco mother of two. In 1994, a Seguin jury assessed him the death penalty for the abduction-rape-murder of 28-year-old Colleen Reed, an Austin accountant. Pamplin's son Larry, the current sheriff of Falls County, appeared at McDuff's Houston trial for the 1992 abduction and murder of Melissa Northrup. "Kenneth McDuff is absolutely the most vicious and savage individual I know," he told reporters. "He has absolutely no conscience, and I think he enjoys killing." If McDuff had been executed as scheduled, he said, "no telling how many lives would have been saved." . . .

His reign of terror finally ended on November 17, 1998, when Kenneth McDuff was put to death by the state of Texas by lethal injection. May his victims rest in peace. . . .

This is why for people who truly value public safety, there is no substitute for . . . capital punishment. It not only forever bars the murderer from killing again, it also prevents parole boards and criminal rights activists from giving him the chance to repeat his crime.

Analyze the essay:

1. What was the chain of events that led to the release of Kenneth McDuff, according to the author?

2. What attributes does Lowe ascribe to what he calls "criminal rights activists"? Why does he view them with disdain?

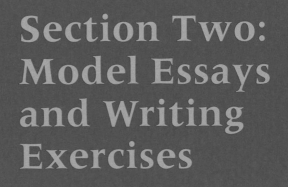

**Section Two:
Model Essays
and Writing
Exercises**

Using Cause and Effect in the Five-Paragraph Essay

The previous section of this book provided you with samples of published persuasive writing on the death penalty. All are persuasive, or opinion, essays making certain arguments about the death penalty. They all also use cause and effect in their arguments. This section will focus on writing your own cause-and-effect essays.

Explaining ideas and events in terms of cause and effect is a common method of organizing essays. Simply put, the *cause* is what makes something happen; the *effect* is what does happen as a result. One way to write (and to spot) cause-and-effect essays is by recognizing the use of certain words that express or signal a cause-and-effect relationship.

A simple example of cause and effect is a car not starting because it is out of gas. The lack of gas is the cause; the failure to start is the effect. Another example of cause-and-effect reasoning is found in Viewpoint One. Bill Kurtis describes how a DNA test on convicted death row inmate Ray Krone established his innocence of the crime. The DNA test was the cause; Crone's exoneration was an effect.

Not all cause-and-effect relationships are as clear-cut as these two examples. It can be difficult to determine the cause of an effect, especially when talking about society-wide causes and effects. For example, smoking tobacco and cancer have been long associated with each other, but not all cancer patients smoked, and not all smokers got cancer. It took decades of debate and research before the U.S. surgeon general concluded in 1964 that smoking cigarettes causes cancer (and even then, that conclusion was disputed by tobacco companies for many years thereafter). In Viewpoint Three Jeff Jacoby notes that the resumption of the death penalty in America in 1977, after a ten-year absence, coincided with drops in the murder rate. His argument is that the death-penalty resumption was a cause; the drop in murder rates an effect. Whether the murder-rate decline is in fact directly attributable to the death penalty or was the effect of other causes is a matter of ongoing debate. Creating and evaluating cause and effect involves both collecting evidence and exercising critical thinking.

In the following section you will read some model essays on the death penalty that use cause-and-effect arguments, and you will do exercises that will help you write your own. To help you, this preface will identify the main components of five-paragraph essays (as well as longer pieces) and discuss how these components fit together. It also will examine the different types of cause-and-effect essays and how they are organized.

Signal or Transition Words Often Found in Cause-and-Effect Essays

because	thus	therefore
so	since	due to
so that	for	this is how
if . . . then	for this reason	accordingly
consequently	as a result of	subsequently

Components of the Five-Paragraph Essay

An *essay* is a short piece of writing that discusses or analyzes one topic. Five-paragraph essays are a form commonly used in school assignments and tests. Every five-paragraph essay begins with an *introduction,* ends with the *conclusion,* and features three *supporting paragraphs* in the middle.

The introduction presents the essay's *topic* and *thesis statement.* The topic is the issue or subject discussed in the essay. All the essays in this book are about the same topic—the death penalty. The thesis or thesis statement is the argument or point that the essay is trying to make about the topic. The essays in this book all have different thesis statements because their arguments about the death penalty differ.

The thesis statement should be a clear statement that tells the reader what the essay will be about. The titles of the viewpoints in this book are good examples; they each present a specific argument or assertion about capital punishment. A focused thesis statement helps determine what will be in the essay; the subsequent paragraphs develop and support its argument.

In addition to presenting the thesis statement, a well-written introductory paragraph captures the attention of the reader and explains why the topic is important. It may provide the reader with background information on the subject matter. It may also "preview" what points will be covered in the following paragraphs.

The introduction is then followed by three (or more) *supporting paragraphs*. These are the main body of the essay. Each paragraph presents and develops a discrete argument (*subtopic*) that supports the essay's thesis statement. Each subtopic is then supported with its own facts, details, and examples. The writer can use various kinds of supporting material and details to back up the topics of each supporting paragraph. These may include statistics, quotations from people with special knowledge or expertise, historic facts, and anecdotes. A rule of writing is that specific and concrete examples are more convincing than vague, general, or unsupported assertions.

The conclusion is the paragraph that closes the essay. Also called the ending or summary paragraph, its function is to summarize or restate the main idea of the essay. It may recall an idea from the introduction or briefly examine the larger implications of the thesis.

Although the order of these component paragraphs is important, one does not have to write the five-paragraph essay in the order it appears. Some writing instructors urge students to decide on a thesis and write the introductory paragraph first. The advantage is that they could then use that paragraph to help structure the rest of the essay. Others suggest that the student could decide on a working thesis, decide on the three points used to support it, and write the supporting paragraphs before writing the introductory and summary paragraphs. That method could be more flexible; if a student researcher finds facts and evidence that go beyond, or even against, the working thesis, then the thesis statement could be reworded.

Types of Cause-and-Effect Essays

Cause-and-effect essays are distinguished by how the thesis and its supporting arguments are organized. There are three types of cause-and-effect essays. The thesis statement of the essay should make it clear what kind of cause-and-effect essay is being written.

In one type, many causes can contribute to a single effect. Supporting paragraphs would each examine one specific cause. For example, Bill Kurtis in Viewpoint One argues that there are several different causes of death penalty–case errors that have resulted in innocent people being sent to death row. The causes he describes include "expectational bias" by the police investigators, a too-cozy relationship between police labs and prosecutors, and ineffective lawyers for the defendants. The ultimate effect of these multiple factors at least in Kurtis's opinion, is the probability that innocent people are being sentenced to death, raising doubt about the reliability of the death-penalty system.

Another type of cause-and-effect essay examines multiple effects from a single cause. The thesis posits that one event or circumstance has multiple results. An example from this volume is found in Viewpoint Two by Paul Rosenzweig. Part of his argument is that abolishing the death penalty would have several negative effects, including the devaluing of the lives of murder victims (and human life in general), murderers escaping their just punishment, and people being killed through the loss of the death penalty's deterrence effect.

A final type of cause-and-effect essay is one that examines a series of causes and effects—a "chain of events" in which each link is both the effect of what happened before and the cause of what happens next. Pat Bane in Viewpoint Six provides one example. A murder (initial cause) creates shock and grief (an effect) in a victim's family and extensive contacts with law enforcement. These contacts then result in a grieving family believing that they will feel better when the criminal justice system runs its course and the murderer is executed. But such raised expectations too often create disappointment and trauma in families when the execution finally happens. Bane concludes that the death penalty is not helpful to victims.

Some Pitfalls to Avoid

In writing argumentative essays about controversial issues such as the death penalty, it is important to remember disputes over cause-and-effect relationships are part of the controversy. The death penalty is a complex phenomenon that has multiple effects and multiple causes, and often there is disagreement over what causes what. One needs to be careful and measured in how arguments are expressed. Avoid overstating cause-and-effect relationships if warranted. Words and phrases such as "it is obvious" and "always" or "never" posit an absolute causal relationship without exception. Use words that qualify the argument, such as "most likely" and "it is possible."

Another pitfall to avoid in writing cause-and-effect essays is to mistake chronology for causation. Just because event X followed event Y does not necessarily mean that X caused Y. Additional evidence may be needed, such as documented studies or similar testimony from many people. Likewise, correlation does not necessarily imply causation. Just because two events happened at the same time does not necessarily mean they are causally related. Again, additional evidence is needed to verify the cause-and-effect argument.

Capital Punishment's Application Is Arbitrary and Unfair

Editor's Notes This first model essay opposes capital punishment. It is structured as a five-paragraph multiple-cause essay. It examines the factors that affect a person's chances of receiving the death penalty. These three factors—the crime's location, the defense attorney, and the race of the victim, are then further examined in the following supporting paragraphs. Each of these paragraphs contains supporting details and information, much of which was taken from the viewpoints in the previous section. The essay then concludes with a summary paragraph that restates the essay's main idea—that the factors affecting who gets the death penalty have little to do with justice or fairness.

As you read this essay, take note of its components and how they are organized (the sidebar notes provide further information on the essay). In addition, consider the following questions:

1. How does the introduction engage the reader's attention?
2. What kinds of supporting evidence are used to back up the essay's arguments?

The first sentence establishes the topic of the essay—the death penalty.

The first two sentences establish a position on capital punishment. The following two sentences beginning with "however" indicate that this opening position is being challenged.

This is the thesis statement for the paragraph and the essay.

The death penalty, according to its proponents, is a just and necessary punishment for those who commit murder. It is the price the murderer must pay for taking another's life. However, the overwhelming majority of murderers do not receive the death penalty. Each year more than fifteen thousand homicides occur in the United States, but fewer than one hundred people are executed. A closer examination of who gets the death penalty reveals that it is comparable to a lottery; those who receive it often are victims of chance circumstances that have little to do with real justice. The factors that increase one's chances of being executed include the location of the crime, the defense lawyer's performance, and the race of the victim.

The location of the crime can have a great bearing on whether one receives the death penalty. First, one must commit a crime in a state that has capital punishment. As of 2004 thirty-eight out of the fifty American states permit capital punishment. Of those thirty eight, ten states—Alabama, Arkansas, Florida, Georgia, Louisiana, Missouri, Oklahoma, South Carolina, Texas, and Virginia—have a much higher death-penalty conviction rate. More than eight out of ten of the nation's executions over the past quarter century have taken place in these ten states. However, receiving the death penalty requires not only committing the crime in the right state, but in the right county. It is the district attorneys working at the county level who decide whether to seek the death penalty and when to prosecute or plea bargain for a lesser sentence. They decide whether to spend the extra money that death-penalty cases often require. Studies have shown that some counties have much higher rates of seeking the death penalty than others with comparable crime problems. Only 15 percent of Texans live in Harris County, but its prosecutors sent enough people to death row to account for 35 percent of the state's death row population. A 1999 study by *USA Today* found that suburban counties send more murderers to death row than urban counties, even though they have lower murder rates. For example, San Mateo County, a suburb of San Francisco, has sent four times as many criminals to death row as San Francisco itself, a city with a greater population and murder rate.

Another important factor in determining who gets executed is the quality of the defense lawyer. Most people who end up on death row tend to be poor and thus unable to afford good legal counsel. They rely instead on marginal private attorneys or on lawyers provided by the state or county. These lawyers often have a large caseload, are relatively underpaid, in some cases have no capital case experience, and in many cases have been found to be less than diligent in defending their clients.

The last sentence in the paragraph previews the topics of the three supporting paragraphs.

This is the topic sentence for the first supporting paragraph.

The discrepancies between states are described in some detail.

Here the essay examines why decisions on the death penalty are made on a county level.

The sentence beginning with "studies have shown" is then followed by some specific examples and statistics.

The word *another* helps in the transition between paragraphs. The paragraph opens with a topic sentence whose argument is then fleshed out.

In 1988, for example, Ronald Keith Williamson was convicted and sentenced to death after his attorney failed to tell the jury that another man had confessed to the crimes (Williamson's conviction was later overturned). According to Steven W. Hawkins, director of the National Coalition to Abolish the Death Penalty, people have been sent to death row after being "represented by drunken lawyers, sleeping lawyers, biased lawyers, inexperienced lawyers, lawyers who were later disbarred, and lawyers who would be institutionalized due to mental illness." Conversely, Supreme Court justice Ruth Bader Ginsburg has observed that "people who are well represented at trial do not get the death penalty."

Yet another factor that influences the death penalty is the race of the murder victim. David Baldus, a University of Iowa scholar, studied twenty-five hundred murder cases in Georgia. He found that defendants accused of killing a white victim are 4.3 times more likely to receive the death penalty than defendants who killed a black victim. His findings have been shown to be true in other states as well. Hawkins notes that "nationwide, just half of murder victims are white, yet four out of every five people executed in the United States have died for killing white people."

So it seems that it takes more than just a simple commission of a crime to get sentenced to death. It helps if one is in a county with a district attorney who enthusiastically supports capital punishment. It helps if one cannot afford a good lawyer. It helps if the victim happens to be white. The significant effects these seemingly irrelevant factors have on the death penalty's application should cause people to question whether capital punishment is fundamentally fair or not.

Create an Outline from an Existing Essay

In many cases it helps to create an outline of the five-paragraph essay before you write it. The outline can help you organize the information, arguments, and evidence you have gathered with your research.

For this exercise, create an outline that could have been used to write the first model essay. This "reverse engineering" exercise is meant to help familiarize you with how outlines can help classify and arrange information.

Part of the outline has already been started to give you an idea of the assignment.

Outline: Write the Essay's Thesis

I. Supporting Argument 1

Location of the crime affects whether one receives the death penalty.

   a. Death penalty vs. non–death penalty states matter.

      1) Thirty-eight states permit capital punishment.

      2) Ten states account for most of the nation's executions.

   b. The county also matters.

      1)

      2)

II. Supporting Argument 2

   a. evidence or elaboration

   b.

   c.

III. Supporting Argument 3

   a.

   b.

   c.

Capital Punishment Helps Society

Editor's Notes   The second essay, also written in five paragraphs, takes a position in support of capital punishment. It is an example of a multiple-effect essay. The thesis—that capital punishment has positive effects on society—is stated at the end of the first paragraph.

The next three paragraphs all present three different benefits that are attributed to the death penalty. As in the first essay, these supporting paragraphs utilize examples and material from the viewpoints in the previous section.

The notes in the sidebar provide questions that will help you analyze how this essay is organized and how it is written.

The first sentence tells the reader that the essay will be about the death penalty. What does the second sentence do?

Where is the thesis statement for the essay found in this paragraph?

Referring back to "citizens" creates a smooth transition from the thesis statement to the first of the supporting paragraphs.

What is the topic sentence for this paragraph?

The writer uses a personal testimonial to support the position stated in the paragraph's topic sentence.

Discussions about the death penalty often focus on death row inmates and whether they deserve to live or die. But the death penalty also affects the society outside the courtroom or execution chamber. In the ongoing debate about capital punishment, it is important to note that the death penalty has significant positive benefits for law-abiding citizens.

Such citizens include those most affected personally by murder—the relatives and friends of murder victims. Many people who have survived the traumatic experience of losing a loved one to murder have found comfort knowing that the person responsible for their loss has been given the ultimate punishment of death. Jack Collins, the father of a murder victim, says the death penalty is "a way of giving the victims and their families a feeling of satisfaction for what was done to them, to make them whole." In some cases viewing the execution firsthand can help people in Collins's situation attain a sense of closure and peace of mind. To expedite this process, sixteen states have passed laws allowing such victims to personally witness the executions of the criminals convicted of killing their loved ones.

The practice of capital punishment also helps all of us by preventing more people from facing Jack Collins's situation—or even becoming the victims of a murder. The death penalty works in several different ways to prevent homicides and make us all a little safer. Convicted murderers sentenced to life in prison have been known to kill again after they have been paroled or have escaped from prison. The death penalty, on the other hand, provides a foolproof way of ensuring that convicted murderers never kill again. In addition, many people argue that criminals fear execution, and that this fear deters criminals who would otherwise kill their victims. Social scientist Isaac Ehrlich has studied the death penalty and calculated that each execution deters seven to eight murders. Newspaper columnist Jeff Jacoby notes that the murder rate doubled between 1965 and 1980, a time when capital punishment was scarcely used. Since then, he remarks, "as executions have become more numerous, murder has declined."

How does this sentence help the essay's transition from the first to the second paragraph? What is the topic sentence for this paragraph?

What are the two different mechanisms by which the death penalty prevents murder that are described in this paragraph?

What authority is cited to support the paragraph's topic argument?

The satisfaction Collins and similar victims express and the added protection the death penalty affords society indicate a deeper reason to support capital punishment. By using the death penalty, society demands that the lives of victims be valued as much or more than the lives of criminals. Collins's daughter was raped and tortured before she was killed. Punishing such horrible crimes with anything less than death amounts to giving murderers more than what their victims received and carries the implicit message that the life of the criminal should be protected more than the life of the victim. The death penalty, says Collins, "shows that society . . . and the entire criminal justice system care enough about us to see to it that our daughter's killer receives his appropriate punishment." The death penalty validates the worth of the lives of murder victims and potential murder victims—in other words, all of us.

What is the topic sentence for this paragraph?

Why do you think the subtopics were presented in the order they were?

How does quoting from someone personally affected by murder and the death penalty lend support to the paragraph's argument?

How does the writer avoid simply repeating the three supporting ideas?

The concluding sentence restates the main thesis in different words—often a good way to close the essay and remind readers of its main argument.

Sparing the lives of people on death row has consequences. Abolishing the death penalty deprives the families of murder victims of seeing their relative's killer punished. It will cause an increase in murders and crime and send a message that society does not value the lives of murder victims as much as criminals. The death penalty is not a barbarous practice that must be stopped but a vital part of the criminal justice system that helps us all.

Exercise Two

Create an Outline for an Opposing Persuasive Essay

The second model essay presents one point of view regarding the death penalty. For this exercise, your assignment is to find supporting ideas, create an outline, and ultimately write a multiple-effect essay that argues an opposing view.

Part I: Using information from some of the eight viewpoints in the previous section, write down three or more arguments that support the following thesis statement: **The death penalty has significant negative consequences for law-abiding citizens.** Each argument should illustrate a distinctive *negative effect* of the death penalty.

For each of the three ideas, write down facts or information that support it, again drawing from the viewpoints in the previous section. These could be:

statistical information
direct quotations from the articles
anecdotes of past events
elaboration of cause-and-effect sequence

Example: The death penalty is causing financial strain on communities.

Average expense of a capital case trial is $2 million [from Bill Kurtis viewpoint].

Legal analyst Bill Kurtis says the death penalty "threatens to bankrupt county budgets in some cases." [Kurtis viewpoint.]

Study in North Carolina found that the death penalty cost $2.16 million more than imprisoning someone for life without parole [Frederick C. Millett viewpoint].

New Jersey had to dismiss five hundred police officers to pay for death-penalty costs, according to Frederick C. Millett.

Millett quotation: "The death penalty is in fact making America a more unsafe place to live, because funds are gong to the death penalty instead of more needed crime-fighting strategies."

Part II: Place the information from Part I in outline form.
Thesis statement: The death penalty has significant negative consequences for law-abiding citizens.
   I. Negative Effect A
      Details and elaboration
   II. Negative Effect B
      Details and elaboration
   III. Negative Effect C
      Details and elaboration

Part III: Write the arguments in paragraph form.
You now have three arguments that support the paragraph's thesis statement, as well as supporting material. Use the outline to write out your three supporting arguments in paragraph form. Each paragraph has a topic sentence that states the paragraph's thesis and supporting sentences that express the facts, details, and examples that support the paragraph's argument. The paragraph may also have a concluding or summary sentence.

A Governor Concludes That the Death Penalty Is Unfair

| **Editor's Notes** | The following essay illustrates the third type of cause-and-effect essay. It illustrates multiple causes of a single event or phenomenon, but the causes are sequential. In other words, instead of factors A, B, and C causing phenomenon X, this third type of essay describes how A causes B, which then causes C, which in turn creates X. This is sometimes known as the domino effect. Chronology—expressing what events come before and which after—plays an important part in this type of essay.

Several other differences exist between this essay and the first two. This essay is more than five paragraphs. Sometimes five paragraphs is simply not enough to adequately develop an idea. It is also different from the others in that most of it focuses not on the death penalty in general but on a single discrete event—the decision of a governor to commute all death sentences in his state. The first paragraph begins with describing the governor's decision and why some people were surprised by it. The second paragraph then goes back in time to when the governor was a death-penalty supporter. The following paragraphs follow a chronological order in describing the series of events that led the governor to his decision.

Some cause-and-effect essays of this third type simply describe a process or event. This essay goes beyond the single event it is describing (and its causes) to make a more general point that the death penalty is unfair and untenable. This can be seen in how it ends. Some might argue it has two concluding paragraphs instead of one. The second-to-last paragraph restates the main events that have been described before and returns to where the essay began—the governor's decision to empty death row. The essay could end here, but it would be more a narrative or expository essay rather than one that put forward an argument. That is accomplished in the last paragraph, when the author draws an opinionated conclusion about the death penalty based on the previous chain of events. Thus, like the first two model essays, this essay makes an argument, then seeks to support it with evidence.

As you read the essay, consider the questions on the side of the page, including those asking to identify the essay's and paragraph's thesis statements.

On January 11, 2003, Governor George Ryan of Illinois used his powers as governor to remove 167 people from death row. He issued pardons to four prisoners he believed were convicted in error and commuted the sentences of others to life without parole. His actions emptied the state's death row and was the largest commutation by a governor in modern U.S. history. The announcement was met with some surprise because Ryan, a conservative Republican, was a death-penalty supporter when he began his term as governor. His dramatic decision to empty death row was the culmination of several events during his term of office as governor—events that convinced him that the death penalty, as administered by the state, cannot be applied fairly.

What is the thesis statement of this paragraph (and essay)?

What phrases in this paragraph indicate that what follows will be a cause-and-effect essay?

In February 1999, weeks after Ryan was first sworn into office, Anthony Porter was released from death row after another man confessed to his crime of double murder. Porter's sentence was officially reversed on March 11, 1999. Porter, who was mentally retarded, had spent sixteen years on death row. At one point in 1998 he came within forty-eight hours of being killed before a legal appeal stopped the execution. His case was investigated by journalism students at Northwestern University; they discovered that a key witness had been pressured by police to testify against him. It was Porter's release, Ryan later recounted, that planted the first doubts about capital punishment in his mind.

What event is described here?

What effects does it have?

Porter's story brought new public attention to the problem of wrongful death-penalty convictions. Reporters for the *Chicago Tribune* launched their own investigation into the state's death-penalty cases. In November 1999 the newspaper published a series of articles about Porter's case and other questionable convictions and problems within Illinois' death-penalty system. These problems included

What is the thesis for this paragraph?

What are some of the supporting facts that relate back to the paragraph thesis?

incompetent defense attorneys who were later disbarred, coerced testimony of witnesses by police, and false or questionable testimony from jailhouse informants. On January 13, 2000, yet another death row inmate, Steve Manning, was released after a state court found that he had been convicted of a crime he did not commit. That brought the total number of such cases since 1977 to thirteen—one more than the number of people actually executed during that time. The questions raised by the newspaper stories and Manning's release strengthened doubts about the system's fairness to many, including Ryan. The governor had earlier decided not to commute the death sentence of a criminal executed in November 1999, but was facing a similar decision on a second prisoner scheduled for execution in early 2000. "I had to ask myself," Ryan recalled in a 2001 speech, "how could I go forward with so many unanswered questions?"

Why do you think this paragraph and the preceding one conclude with a focus on what Ryan is thinking?

What cause-and-effect chain of events is described in this paragraph?

Ryan responded to these concerns about capital punishment on January 31, 2000, by imposing a moratorium on the death penalty in Illinois. He told the people of Illinois that he was worried about the possibility of innocent people being executed and that he would not approve any more executions until the entire death-penalty structure had been reviewed. On March 9, 2000, Ryan announced he was forming a commission to study Illinois' death-penalty system and to recommend reforms. The commission's fourteen members included nine former prosecutors and a former U.S. senator. Over the next two years the commission held public hearings, met in private sessions with families and murder victims, and reviewed Illinois' death-penalty laws.

How do the events described here develop or support the thesis for the essay as expressed in the opening paragraph?

Why are dates continually brought up in this essay?

In April 2002 the commission issued its final report. They concluded that the laws and administrative structure governing the state's death penalty were severely flawed and made eighty-five specific recommendations to fix it. These included banning the execution of the mentally retarded, establishing an independent forensics center to evaluate evidence, reducing the number of crimes punishable by death, and videotaping police interrogations. However, the commission also concluded that even if all of its reforms were adopt-

What is this paragraph's topic sentence?

ed, there was no 100 percent guarantee that an innocent person would never be executed.

Governor Ryan subsequently attempted to get the Illinois legislature to pass the commission's recommended reforms. However, many elected prosecutors and district attorneys fought the reforms, arguing that changes would limit their ability to impose the death penalty. Three times the legislature turned down a chance to adopt the commission's recommendations. "The system is as bad today as it was three years ago," asserted Dennis Culloton, Ryan's press secretary, in January 2003. Ryan, who had chosen not to run for reelection, faced the prospect of leaving office with no reforms in the death-penalty system and the possibility that a future governor would end his moratorium.

What is the usefulness of the word *subsequently* for cause-and-effect essays?

Ultimately, it was the question of fairness first raised by Porter's release, then highlighted by newspaper reports and examined by the commission, that inspired Ryan's decision to commute all of Illinois' death row population. He made his announcement three days before leaving office. "Because our three-year study has found only more questions about the fairness of the sentencing; because of the spectacular failure to reform the system; because we have seen justice delayed for countless death row inmates with potentially meritorious claims; because the Illinois death penalty system is arbitrary and capricious—and therefore immoral—I no longer shall tinker with the machinery of death," Ryan said in his January 11, 2003, speech announcing his decision. "Our capital system is haunted by the demon of error—error in determining guilt, and error in determining who among the guilty deserves to die. Because of all of these reasons today I am commuting the sentences of all death row inmates."

How is the essay's thesis restated in this paragraph?

The story of Ryan's conversion from being a death-penalty supporter to a person who stopped 167 executions can teach us something important about the death-penalty debate. Public opinion polls show that the majority of Americans support capital punishment—at least in theory. But few Americans feel the responsibility of holding the life-and-death power that Ryan had over death row prisoners,

What is the topic of this paragraph? How does it relate to the rest of the essay?

and few have spent as much time and effort as Ryan did in examining how the criminal justice system decides who lives and who dies. If more Americans took responsibility for seriously thinking about capital punishment as it exists in this country today, perhaps more would agree with Ryan that the death penalty is fundamentally unfair and should be discontinued.

Exercise Three | Evaluating and Writing Introductory and Concluding Paragraphs

The introductory and concluding paragraphs can greatly improve an essay by quickly imparting to the reader the essay's main idea. Well-written introductions not only present the essay's thesis statement but also grab the attention of the reader and tell why the topic being explored is important and interesting. The conclusion reiterates the thesis statement but also is the last chance for the writer to make an impression on the reader and to drive home his or her argument.

The Introduction

There are several techniques to choose from to attract the reader's attention in the opening paragraph. An essay can start with

- an anecdote: A brief story that illustrates a point relevant to the topic.
- startling information: True and pertinent facts or statistics that illustrate the point of the essay. A brief opening assertion can then be elaborated upon over the next few sentences.
- setting up and knocking down a position: Beginning the essay with an assertion proponents of one side of a controversy believe, only to then raise questions about that assertion.
- summary information: The first sentence or two introduces the topic in general terms, then each sentence becomes gradually more specific until the concluding sentence, which is the thesis statement.

Remember that in a cause-and-effect essay, the introductory paragraph should establish the cause that is being examined (for its multiple effects) or the effect that is being examined (for its multiple and/or chain-of-event causes).

Assignment One: Reread the introductory paragraphs of the model essays and of the eight viewpoints in the previous section. Identify which of the techniques described above are used in the example essays. How else do they get the attention of the reader while presenting the thesis statement of the essay?

Assignment Two: Write an introduction for the essay you have outlined and partially written from Exercise Two. You can use one of the techniques described above.

The Conclusion

The conclusion brings the essay to a close by summarizing or restating its main argument(s). Good conclusions go beyond simply repeating the argument, however. They also answer the reader's question of "so what?"—in other words, they tell why the argument is important to consider. Some conclusions may also explore the broader implications of the thesis argument. They may close with a quotation or refer back to an anecdote or event in the essay. In essays on controversial topics, such as the death penalty, the conclusion should reiterate which side the essay is taking.

Assignment Three: Reread the concluding paragraphs of the model essays and of the eight viewpoints in the previous section. Which were most effective in driving their arguments home to the reader? What sort of devices did they use?

Assignment Four: Write a conclusion for the essay you have outlined and partially written in Exercise Two.

Assignment Five: Review the five-paragraph essay you have just written.

Writing a Cause-and-Effect Five-Paragraph Essay

The final exercise is to write your own five-paragraph cause-and-effect essay that either supports or opposes capital punishment. You can use the resources in this book for information about both the death penalty and how to structure a cause-and-effect essay.

The following steps are suggestions on how to approach this assignment.

Step One: Decide on the topic.
For this exercise, the topic is the death penalty or some particular aspect of the death penalty.

Possible topics include:

> executing juveniles
> erroneous death penalty convictions
> public attitudes toward the death penalty
> televising executions
> the financial costs of the death penalty
> the morality of the death penalty

Step Two: Write down questions and answers about the topic.
Possible questions include:

> Why is this topic important?
> Why should people be interested in this topic?
> What question am I going to answer in this paragraph or essay?
> How can I best answer this question?
> What facts or ideas can I use to support the answer to my question?
> Will the question's answer either support or oppose the death penalty?
> How can I make this essay interesting to the reader?

Questions especially for cause-and-effect essays include:

What are the causes of the topic being examined?

What are the effects of the topic being examined?

Are there single or multiple causes?

Are there single or multiple effects?

Is a chain reaction or domino series of events involved?

Step Three: Gather facts and ideas related to your essay topic.

This volume contains several places to find information, including the viewpoints and the appendices. In addition, you may want to research the books, articles, and Web sites listed, or do additional research in your local library. If you are using direct quotations or statements of other people, it is usually important to note their qualifications and possible biases.

Step Four: Develop a workable thesis statement.

Use what you have written down in steps two and three to help you choose the point you want to make in your essay.

Remember that the thesis statement has two parts: the topic (death penalty) and the point of the essay. It should be expressed in a clear sentence and make an arguable point. For cause-and-effect essays, the thesis should indicate the cause or effect being examined.

Examples:

Executing juveniles harms society.

This could be a multiple-effect essay that examines the effects killing juveniles has on society.

Legal safeguards in the criminal justice system prevent the execution of innocents.

This can be the basis for a multiple-cause essay:

The legal protections built into the criminal justice system (the causes) are enough to prevent people from being executed by mistake (the effect).

Step Five: Write an outline or diagram.

1. Write the thesis statement at the top.
2. Write roman numerals I, II, and III on the left side of the page.
3. Next to each roman numeral, write down the best arguments you came up with in Step Three. These should all directly relate to and support the thesis statement. If the essay is a multiple-cause essay, write down three causes; if it is a multiple-effect essay, write down three effects. If it is a domino chain organization, write down the chain of events in sequence.
4. Next to each letter write down facts or information that support that particular idea.
5. An alternative to the roman numeral outline is the diagram (see box).

Diagrams: An Alternative to Outlines

Some students might prefer a different way of organizing their ideas than the roman numeral outline. An alternative method of organizing ideas on paper is the diagram. A possible approach would be as follows:

1. Draw a circle in the middle of the page. In that circle, write the topic of the essay.
2. Draw three or four lines out from the circle. Draw additional circles at the end of the lines.
3. In each circle write some arguments or points about the topic.
4. Draw three or four lines out of each outer circle and place more circles at the ends of those lines.
5. In each new circle write some facts or information that support that particular idea.

Step Six: Write the three supporting paragraphs.
Use your outline to write the three supporting paragraphs. Write down the main point in sentence form. Do the same for the supporting points of information. Each sentence should support the topic of the paragraph. Sometimes (not always), paragraphs include a conclusion or summary sentence that restates the paragraph's argument.

Step Seven: Write the introduction and conclusion. See Exercise Three for information on writing introductions and conclusions.

Step Eight: Read and rewrite.
Does the essay maintain a consistent tone?
Do all sentences in some fashion reinforce your general thesis?
Do paragraphs flow from one to the other? Do you need transition words or phrases?
Is there a sense of progression—does each paragraph advance the argument by offering more information than preceding paragraphs?
Are there any spelling or grammatical errors?
Does the essay get bogged down in too much detail or irrelevant material?

Tips on Writing Effective Cause-and-Effect Essays
You do not need to describe *every* possible cause of an event or phenomenon. Focus on the most important ones.

- Write in the active, not passive, voice.

- Vary your sentence structure, especially in stating and restating your thesis.

- Maintain a professional, reasonable tone of voice. Avoid sounding too uncertain or insulting.

- Anticipate what the reader's counterarguments may be and answer them.

- Use sources which state facts and evidence.

- Do not write in the first person.

- Avoid assumptions or generalizations without evidence.

Section Three: Supporting Research Material

Facts About the Death Penalty

The Death Penalty in the United States

- America's first recorded execution took place in Jamestown, Virginia, in 1608.
- In 1846 Michigan became the first state to abolish the death penalty. Rhode Island abolished it in 1852, followed by Wisconsin in 1853.
- A federal moratorium was imposed on the death penalty from 1967 to 1976, during which time no one was executed in the United States.
- From 1977 to 2004, 944 people have been executed in the United States; 54 percent of them were white, 34 percent were black.
- Ten females have been executed in the United States since 1977. As of 2002 there were fifty-one American women on death row.
- Of the 944 people executed in the United States since 1977, 22 were under the age of eighteen at the time of their capital crime.
- The death penalty is allowable under federal military and civilian law. In June 2001 Oklahama City bomber Timothy McVeigh became the first federal prisoner executed since 1963.
- Thirty-eight states presently provide for capital punishment. The twelve states with no death penalty are Alaska, Hawaii, Iowa, Maine, Massachusetts, Michigan, Minnesota, North Dakota, Rhode Island, Vermont, West Virginia, and Wisconsin.
- Of the states that permit the death penalty, Texas uses the death penalty the most. It has executed 336 people since 1977. Virginia is next with 94 executions; then Oklahoma, with 75; Missouri, 61; and Florida, which has executed 59 people since 1977.
- Of the states that permit the death penalty, Colorado, Idaho, New Mexico, Tennessee, and Wyoming use the

death penalty least often. Since 1977 they have each put one person to death.

- In the thirty-eight states that enacted the death penalty, five different methods of execution are legal: lethal injection, electrocution, lethal gas, firing squad, and hanging. Lethal injection is the most common form of execution, accounting for 744 executions or 81 percent of the total since 1977. Since 1977, 152 criminals have been executed by electric chair, 11 by gas chamber, 3 by hanging, and 2 by firing squad.

- In some states the method of execution depends on when the crime was committed. For example, in Georgia an inmate may be executed by electrocution if they committed their crime prior to May 1, 2000. If they committed their crime after this date they will die by lethal injection.

- In some states, such as Arizona or California, inmates may elect whether they are executed by lethal injection or lethal gas. In Arizona an inmate may have the option of choosing between electrocution and lethal injection.

- Over two thousand of America's death row inmates have been awaiting execution for more than six years.

- Each state has different rules regarding who can witness an execution. In Oregon the immediate family of the victim, including parents, spouse, siblings, children, and grandparents, can watch an execution. In North Carolina, witnesses are limited to two people from the victim's family. In Georgia no witnesses are allowed.

- In 2002 the U.S. Supreme Court barred the execution of mentally retarded offenders, overturning its 1989 ruling on the matter. Also in the same year the Court ruled that the death penalty must be imposed through a finding of a jury and not a judge.

- According to the Death Penalty Information Center, since 1982 thirty-six executions have had complications, including the person being executed catching on fire, experiencing violent spasms, heavy bleeding from the face, choking, or other complications that resulted in a prolonged death.

Facts Compiled by Amnesty International on the Death Penalty Around the World

- The United States is among seventy-eight countries that use the death penalty as punishment for crime.
- In 2003, 84 percent of all known executions occurred in China, Iran, Vietnam, and the United States.
- Since 1990 the countries that have executed juvenile offenders include China, the Democratic Republic of Congo, Iran, Nigeria, Pakistan, Saudi Arabia, the United States, and Yemen. Of these, the United States has carried out the most executions of juvenile offenders, nineteen since 1990.
- Of the countries that allow the death penalty, 5 use lethal injection (the most common form of execution in the United States), 75 use firing squads, 59 use hanging, 6 use stoning, and 3 use beheading (Congo, Saudi Arabia, and United Arab Emirates).
- Canada, Australia, and most of Europe have abolished the death penalty for all crimes.

The Death Penalty in American Public Opinion

According to a Gallup poll taken in May 2004:

- Of those surveyed, 62 percent did not believe the death penalty was a deterrent to committing murder, yet 71 percent supported executing a person convicted of homicide.
- Of those surveyed, 50 percent thought the death penalty was a better punishment for murder over life in prison; 46 percent said they thought life in prison was a more appropriate penalty for murder.
- Of those surveyed, 23 percent said the death penalty was imposed too often, 25 percent said it was imposed appropriately, and 48 percent said the death penalty was not imposed often enough.
- Of those surveyed, 55 percent said they believed the death penalty was applied fairly, while 39 percent said they believed it was applied unfairly.

Finding and Using Sources of Information

When you write a cause-and-effect or other form of persuasive essay, it is usually necessary to find information to support your point of view. You can use sources such as books, magazine articles, and online articles.

Using Books and Articles

You can find books and articles in a library by using the cataloging system. If you are not sure how to use the card catalog or the library's computer, ask a librarian to instruct you. You can also use a computer to find many magazine articles and other articles written specifically for the Internet.

You are likely to find a lot more information than you can possibly use in your essay, so your first task is to narrow it down to what is likely to be most usable. Look at book and article titles. Look at book chapter titles, and take a look at the book index to see if the book contains information on the specific topic you want to write about. (For example, if you want to write about the execution of juveniles and you find a book about capital punishment, check the chapter titles and index to be sure it contains information about the juveniles before you bother to check out the book.)

For a five-paragraph essay, you do not need a great deal of supporting information, so quickly try to narrow down your materials to a few good books and magazine or Internet articles. You do not need dozens. You might even find that one or two good books or articles contain all the information you need.

You probably do not have time to read an entire book, so find the chapters or sections that relate to your topic, and skim these. When you find useful information, copy it onto a notecard or notebook. You should look for supporting facts, statistics, quotations, and examples.

Evaluate the Source

When you select your supporting information, it is important that you evaluate its source. This is especially important with information you find on the Internet. Because nearly anyone can put information on the Internet, there is as much bad information as good information. Before using Internet information—or any information—try to determine if the source seems to be reliable. Is the author or Internet site sponsored by a legitimate organization? Is it from a government source? Does the author have any special knowledge or training relating to the topic you are looking up? Does the article give any indication of where its information comes from?

Using Your Supporting Information

When you use supporting information from a book, article, interview, or other source, there are three important things to remember:

1. Make it clear whether you are using a direct quotation or a paraphrase. If you copy information directly from your source, you are quoting it. You must put quotation marks around the information, and tell where the information comes from. If you put the information in your own words, you are paraphrasing it. Sometimes you must tell where you got this information, too. (See number 3, "Give credit where credit is due.")

Here is an example of using a quotation:

> According to Human Rights Watch, a private organization that promotes respect for political and civil rights, "innocent people with mental retardation all too often confess to capital crimes they did not commit, simply because they want to give the 'right' answer to a police officer, or because they believe that if the police say they did something, they must have done it, even if they do not remember."[1]

1. Human Rights Watch, "The Miscarriage of Justice: Mental Retardation and Capital Trials," www.hrw.org, March 2001.

Here is an example of a brief paraphrase of the same passage:

According to Human Rights Watch, a private organization that promotes respect for political and civil rights, mentally retarded people often believe whatever the police accuse them of doing, and end up confessing to capital crimes they never committed.

2. Use the information fairly. Be careful to use supporting information in the way the author intended it. There is a joke that movie ads containing critics' comments like "First-Class!" "Best ever!" and other glowing phrases take them from longer reviews that said something like "This movie is first-class trash" or "This movie is this director's best ever—and that isn't saying much!" This is called taking information out of context (using it in a way the original writer did not intend). This is using supporting evidence unfairly.

3. Give credit where credit is due. You must give credit when you use someone else's information, but not every piece of supporting information needs a credit.

- If the supporting information is general knowledge— that is, it can be found in many sources—you do not have to cite (give credit to) your source.
- If you directly quote a source, you must give credit.
- If you paraphrase information from a specific source, you must give credit.

If you do not give credit where you should, you are plagiarizing—or stealing—someone else's work.

Giving Credit

There are a number of ways to give credit. Your teacher will probably want you to do it one of three ways:

- Informal: As in the examples in number 1 above, you tell where you got the information in the same place you use it.

- Informal list: At the end of the article, place an unnumbered list of the sources you used. This tells the reader where, in general, you got your information, but it does not tell specifically where you got any single fact.

- Formal: Use a footnote, like the first example in number 1 above. (A footnote is generally placed at the end of an article or essay, although it may be located in different places depending on your teacher's requirements.)

Your teacher will tell you exactly how information should be credited in your essay. Generally, the very least information needed is the original author's name and the name of the article or other publication.

Be sure you know exactly what information your teacher requires before you start looking for your supporting information so that you know what information to include with your notes.

Sample Essay Topics

Cause-and-Effect Essays

America's Death Penalty System Executes Innocent People

The Death Penalty for Juveniles Deters Juvenile Crime

The Death Penalty for Juveniles Does Not Deter Juvenile Crime

Legal Appeals Make the Death Penalty System Too Slow

America's Retention of the Death Penalty Isolates It from Other Countries

Public Attitudes Toward Capital Punishment Are Shaped by Fears of Crime

The Death Penalty Makes People More Callous

The Death Penalty Restores Respect for the Rule of Law

The Death Penalty Can Save Taxpayer Money

The Death Penalty Costs Taxpayer Money

Racism Affects How the Death Penalty Is Carried Out

Sexism Affects How the Death Penalty Is Carried Out

Methods of Execution Cause Unnecessary Pain and Suffering

Televising Executions Would Help Deter Crime

Televising Executions Would Harm Society

DNA Evidence Could Help Prevent the Execution of Innocents

DNA Evidence Will Not Prevent the Execution of Innocents

General Persuasive Essays

The Death Penalty Is Moral

The Death Penalty Is Immoral

The Death Penalty for Juveniles Is Fair

The Death Penalty for Juveniles Is Unfair

Executing the Mentally Retarded Is Fair

Executing the Mentally Retarded Is Not Fair

Death Row Prisoners Are Treated Humanely

Life Imprisonment Is More Cruel than Capital Punishment

The Death Penalty Should Be Used with Greater Frequency

The Death Penalty Should Be Abolished

Organizations to Contact

American Civil Liberties Union (ACLU)
125 Broad St., 18th Floor, New York, NY 10004
(212) 549-2500 • fax: (212) 549-2646
Web site: www.aclu.org

The ACLU believes that capital punishment violates the Constitution's ban on cruel and unusual punishment as well as the requirements of due process and equal protection under the law.

Amnesty International USA (AI)
322 Eighth Ave., New York, NY 10001
(212) 807-8400 • fax: (212) 627-1451
Web site: www.amnesty-usa.org

Amnesty International is an independent worldwide human rights movement. AI's Program to Abolish the Death Penalty (PADP) coordinates efforts to build coalitions with grassroots activists and social justice organizations working toward the elimination of the death penalty worldwide.

Canadian Coalition Against the Death Penalty (CCADP)
PO Box 38104, 550 Eglinton Ave. West
Toronto, ON M5N 3A8 Canada
(416) 693-9112 • fax: (416) 686-1630
e-mail: info@ccadp.org • Web site: www.ccadp.org

CCADP is a not-for-profit international human rights organization dedicated to educating the public on alternatives to the death penalty worldwide and to providing emotional and practical support to death row inmates, their families, and the families of murder victims.

Criminal Justice Legal Foundation (CJLF)
PO Box 1199, Sacramento, CA 95816
(916) 446-0345

e-mail: cjlf@cjlf.org • Web site: www.cjlf.org

The CJLF seeks to restore a balance between the rights of crime victims and the criminally accused. The foundation supports the death penalty and works to reduce the length, complexity, and expense of appeals as well as to improve law enforcement's ability to identify and prosecute criminals.

Death Penalty Focus
870 Market St., Suite 859, San Francisco, CA 94102
(415) 243-0143 • fax: (415) 243-0994
e-mail: info@deathpenalty.org
Web site: www.deathpenalty.org

Founded in 1988, Death Penalty Focus is a nonprofit organization dedicated to the abolition of capital punishment through grassroots organization, research, and the dissemination of information about the death penalty and its alternatives.

Death Penalty Information Center (DPIC)
1326 Eighteenth St. NW, 5th Floor, Washington, DC 20036
(202) 293-6970 • fax: (202) 822-4787
e-mail: dpic@deathpenaltyinfo.org
Web site: www.deathpenaltyinfo.org

DPIC conducts research into public opinion on the death penalty. The center believes capital punishment is discriminatory and excessively costly and that it may result in the execution of innocent persons.

Justice for All (JFA)
(713) 935-9300
e-mail: info@jfa.net • Web site: www.jfa.net

Justice for All is a not-for-profit criminal justice reform organization that supports the death penalty. It publishes the monthly newsletter *Voice of Justice* and also manages the Web sites www.murdervictims.com and www.prodeath penalty.com.

Lamp of Hope Project

PO Box 305, League City, TX 77574-0305
e-mail: ksebung@lampofhope.org
Web site: www.lampofhope.org

The project was established and is run primarily by Texas death row inmates. Its goals include educating the public about the death penalty and its alternatives and supporting victims' families by promoting healing and reconciliation.

National Coalition to Abolish the Death Penalty (NCADP)

920 Pennsylvania Ave. SE, Washington, DC 20003
(202) 543-9577 • fax: (202) 543-7798
e-mail: kjones@ncadp.org • Web site: www.ncadp.org

The National Coalition to Abolish the Death Penalty is a collection of more than 115 groups working together to stop executions in the United States. The organization compiles statistics on the death penalty and publishes information packets, pamphlets, and research materials.

Bibliography

Books

Antoinette Bosco, *Choosing Mercy: A Mother of Murder Victims Pleads to End the Death Penalty.* Maryknoll, NY: Orbis, 2001.

Stanley Cohen, *The Wrong Men: America's Epidemic of Wrongful Death Row Convictions.* New York: Carroll & Graf, 2003.

L. Kay Gillespie, *Executions and the Execution Process: Questions and Answers.* Boston: Allyn and Bacon, 2002.

Mike Gray, *The Death Game: Capital Punishment and the Luck of the Draw.* Monroe, ME: Common Courage, 2003.

Harry Henderson, *Capital Punishment.* New York: Facts On File, 2000.

Jesse L. Jackson Sr., Jesse L. Jackson Jr., and Bruce Shapiro, *Legal Lynching: The Death Penalty and America's Future.* New York: New Press, 2001.

Bill Kurtis, *The Death Penalty on Trial: Crisis in American Justice.* New York: Public Affairs, 2004.

Ann Chih Lin, ed., *Capital Punishment.* Washington, DC: CQ Press, 2002.

Dan Malone and Howard Swindle, *America's Condemned: Death Row Inmates in Their Own Words.* Kansas City, MO: Andrews McMeel, 1999.

Lane Nelson and Burk Foster, eds., *Death Watch: A Death Penalty Anthology.* Upper Saddle River, NJ: Prentice-Hall, 2001.

Helen Prejean, *The Death of Innocents: An Eyewitness Account of Wrongful Executions.* New York: Random House, 2004.

Barry Scheck, Peter Neufeld, and Jim Dwyer, *Actual Innocence: Five Days to Execution and Other Dispatches from the Wrongly Convicted.* New York: Doubleday, 2000.

Scott Turow, *Ultimate Punishment: A Lawyer's Reflections on Dealing with the Death Penalty.* New York: Farrar, Straus and Giroux, 2003.

Periodicals

Hugo Adam Bedau, "Death's Dwindling Dominion," *American Prospect,* July 2004.

Peter L. Berger, "Beyond the 'Humanly Tolerable,'" *National Review,* July 17, 2000.

Walter Berns, "Where Are the Death Penalty Critics Today?" *Wall Street Journal,* June 11, 2001.

Carl M. Cannon, "The Problem with the Chair—a Conservative Case Against Capital Punishment," *National Review,* June 19, 2000.

Current Events, "A Time to Kill? Supreme Court Tackles Death Penalty for Teens," November 19, 2004.

John Dart, "Executing Justice," *Christian Century,* February 13, 2002.

Gregg Easterbrook, "The Myth of Fingerprints: DNA and the End of Innocence," *New Republic,* July 31, 2000.

Thomas R. Eddlem, "10 Anti–Death Penalty Fallacies," *New American,* July 3, 2002.

Robert Grant, "Capital Punishment and Violence," *Humanist,* January/February 2004.

Marc Klaas, "I'll Be There to Watch My 12-Year-Old Daughter's Murderer Go Down," *Newsweek,* June 12, 2000.

Eugene H. Methvin, "Death Penalty Is Fairer than Ever," *Wall Street Journal,* May 10, 2000.

Christina Swarns, "The Uneven Scales of Capital Justice: How Race and Class Affect Who Ends Up on Death Row," *American Prospect,* July 2004.

William Tucker, "The Chair Deters," *National Review,* July 17, 2000.

James Q. Wilson, "What Death Penalty Errors?" *New York Times,* July 10, 2000.

Lewis Yablonsky, "A Road into Minds of Murderers," *Los Angeles Times,* January 14, 2003.

Index

Picture Credits

About the Editor

William Dudley received his BA degree from Beloit College in Wisconsin, where he majored in English composition and wrote for the school newspaper and literary journal. He has since written and published op-ed pieces, travel articles, and other pieces of writing. He has edited dozens of books on history and social issues for Greenhaven Press at Thomson/Gale.